Operation Eternal Freedom
Finding our Freedom in Christ

David K. Trogdon
Chaplain (LTC), USA, Ret.

This book was printed in the United States of America.

To order additional copies of this book contact:
armysoldier79@yahoo.com
850-896-4868

FWB
Publications

Columbus, Ohio

Contents

The Fight for Freedom 5
Welcome to Operation Eternal Freedom..7
Enlistment/Reenlistment... 11
Under Attack......... 15
Our Battle Plan......... 19
Got Faith? 23
Army Life..27
R&R Rewind & Review..31
Why Are We Here? 35
The War is Already Won 39
Winning by Losing..43
Guard Duty..47
Know Your Enemy (Part 1).......... 51
Know Your Enemy (Part 2) 55
R&R Rewind & Review..59
Full Battle Rattle......... 61
Shock and Awe 65
Overcoming Adversity...69
No Weekend Warriors.......... 73
Baghdad Bob..77
This is Buffalo Shepherd, Over...81
R&R Rewind & Review..85
Light in the Dark...87
Clean Your Weapon..91
Spiritual Combat Team..95
Medic!..99
Keep Up the Fight..103
Homecoming...107
R&R Rewind & Review...113
Military Photos...115

David K Trogdon
Chaplain (LTC), USA, Ret.

The Fight for Freedom

"Freedom"

1. "The power or right to act, speak, or think as one wants without hindrance or restraint."
2. "The absence of subjection to foreign domination or despotic government."
3. "The state of not being imprisoned or enslaved."

These three online definitions of "freedom" illustrate that freedom may have different meanings depending on our circumstances. In fact, one may feel free to do and say whatever they want, without any hindrance or restraint, enjoy political freedom and not be enslaved in some far away land and yet still not be free. The opposite can be true. One may live with a life of restraint, live in a place with a despotic government and be imprisoned and yet be freer than many who live in the USA. True freedom is not based on our circumstances but based on our relationship with Christ. The best definition of freedom is found in God's Word. Let's examine the following Scriptures to see what God Himself has to say about true freedom, eternal freedom:

1. John 8:31-36

2. Romans 8:1-4

3. Galatians 5:1

Why Operation Eternal Freedom?

As a Chaplain and Soldier, I was blessed to serve "God and Country" as well as Soldiers and Families for many years. My service included 3 years in Kuwait, Africa, Iraq and Afghanistan as part of Operation Iraqi Freedom (OIF) and Operation Enduring Freedom (OEF). Both of these combat missions cost thousands of lives in the fight for freedom, freedom from terrorism and freedom from oppression. With all the loss of life and sacrifices made by our military and our Families, I can't say if there is much hope for either Iraq or Afghanistan to be free. Instead, we see many, like myself, struggling with PTSD, Traumatic Brain Injuries (TBIs), suicide, depression and numerous addictions. In our quest for freedom for others, many have become enslaved. My heart continually breaks as I hear of another Veteran who has lost their fight for freedom ending their own lives in a desperate measure to try to end the pain. It's not just the Combat Vet, First Responder or Family member who is hurting. Millions today, in their quest for freedom, end up enslaved. This is why I wrote Operation Eternal Freedom and I pray, in some way, it can help you find the true freedom we can only find in Christ.

Welcome to Operation Eternal Freedom!

"If the Son has set you free you shall be free indeed." For those of us who struggle with PTSD, depression, fear, addictions, unhealthy habits, a painful past, guilt, bad relationships, suicidal thoughts or other negative feelings in our lives, the words of Jesus promising freedom may seem to us like an impossibility or an empty promise. The promise of freedom Jesus makes is not just for those "super Christians" who have it all together and who seem to never struggle, fall, fail or hurt. The freedom which only Christ can give is a promise of freedom for everyone who comes to him in faith, no matter who they are, what they have done, or what baggage they may bring. Yes! That includes you! You are not reading this by accident, but by divine appointment. You know you have problems, but God wants you to know and experience His power that can make a difference in any life, including yours. So, welcome to Operation Eternal Freedom and welcome home!

Operation Eternal Freedom is a daily personal study that can help you find and enjoy spiritual freedom in Christ. For the next four weeks we will be examining and applying spiritual truths that can truly make a difference and change your life, not just for today, but for eternity! Each day includes a short lesson, Scripture passages to read, questions for application (Battle Drills), suggestions for prayer (Commo Check), and a MRE (Manna Ready to Enjoy) daily devotional. This 28-day study is based upon 4 spiritual keys that can help unlock whatever is keeping us bound. These keys are: Faith (days 4-10), Resisting the Devil (days 11-17), Experiencing God (days 18-22), and Encouraging Others (days 23-28). We will use the acronym "FREE" to help us remember these keys. Operation Eternal Freedom comes from a soldier's perspective and is for every Christian soldier who fights in the spiritual war on terror every day against the world's worst terrorist, the devil. So, let's move out and don't worry, Jesus is on the point!

BATTLE DRILLS: Luke 15:11-24

Jesus continued: There was a man who had two sons. The younger one said to his father, Father, give me my share of the estate. So he divided his property between them. Not long after that, the younger son got together all he had, set off for a distant country and there squandered his wealth in wild living. After he had spent everything, there was a severe famine in that whole country, and he began to be in need. So he went and hired himself out to a citizen of that country, who sent him to his fields to feed pigs. He longed to fill his stomach with the pods that the pigs were eating, but no one gave him anything. When he came to his senses, he said, how many of my father's hired men have food to spare, and here I am starving to death! I will set out and go back to my father and say to him: Father, I have sinned against heaven and against you. I am no longer worthy to be called your son; make me like one of your hired men. So he got up and went to his father. But while he was still a long way off, his father saw him and was filled with compassion for him; he ran to his son, threw his arms around him and kissed him. The son said to him, Father, I have sinned against heaven and against you. I am no longer worthy to be called your son. But the father said to his servants, Quick! Bring the best robe and put it on him. Put a ring on his finger and sandals on his feet. Bring the fattened calf and kill it. Let's have a feast and celebrate. For this son of mine was dead and is alive again; he was lost and is found. So they began to celebrate.

1.   **In what ways have I acted like the son?**

2.   **What does this passage teach me about God as my Father?**

COMMO CHECK:

Prayer is simply talking to God and telling Him what is on your heart and what you need. Talk to God and ask Him to help you come to know Him better as your Heavenly Father.

My prayer: "My Heavenly Father, I thank you for loving me and for looking and waiting for me to come home to you. Please forgive me for running away from you and your love. Thank you for providing for my forgiveness, my freedom and my future. Please help me during these next 28 days to learn about your freedom and help me to live in your freedom. Thank you for giving me a new life. In Jesus' name, Amen."

MRE (Manna Ready to Enjoy): "Dear Prodigal"

Dear Prodigal,

I want you to know that I still love you. I am waiting for you to come back home. I keep watching, hoping to see you come walking up that long, dusty road. It seems like forever that you have been gone. My heart breaks when I think of you out there all alone. I know you're hurting, I know your sin, and yet I want you to know I still love you. More than anything, I long to take you back into my arms and wipe away your tears. I don't care what you have done, how far you have fallen or how dirty you may be. I have already forgiven you, paid your debt and I will wash you and make you clean. You are MY child and nothing can ever change that. My love for you is unchangeable, unfathomable and unconditional. I don't want to punish you, I don't want you to punish yourself, nor do I want you to try to repay a debt you cannot even begin to pay; a debt which I have already paid for you. I don't want you to suffer, to sacrifice or to be afraid. I just want you to come home. I miss you and I will always love you. Please come home soon.

Love,

Your Heavenly Father

Whether you believe it or not or not, deserve it or not, through Christ, you are God's precious child. He loves you with an everlasting love and will always love you. Don't let fear, shame, or guilt keep you away from the One who will always love you, always forgive you and always take you back into His arms. Simply wake up, get up and go home to your Father! He is waiting for you!

DAVID K. TROGDON, CHAPLAIN AND SOLDIER

Enlistment/Reenlistment
(F-Faith)

People join the military for many reasons. The first time I joined the Army, I was 17-years-old and wanted to get away from a bad home situation and because I wanted a change. The second time, I was 39-years-old and wanted to minister to soldiers and serve my country as an Army chaplain. Some join the military for college funding, economic reasons, career reasons, and a few because they "are tired of mom and dad telling them what to do." Others join the Army because they, too, want to serve their country and do their part, perhaps as parents and grandparents had done name....

After 9-11, the vast majority of young men and women joined knowing that we were a nation at war and were willing to fight and even die, to protect our nation from the threat of terror. After 9-11, patriotism, courage, and determination and anger caused the line at the recruiting stations to swell with volunteers who were willing to leave the comforts of home for an uncertain future and the possibility of combat.

We are at war. Your life is under attack. Satan, the ultimate terrorist, is out to destroy your life, control your mind and rob you of enjoying the freedom that Christ purchased with His own blood. So what do you do? Do you ignore Satan's terrorist attacks, and hope he will leave you alone like so many who hope we can negotiate with terrorists or just "coexist." Do you put all your trust in the wisdom and advice of counselors, your Facebook friends or in others who also struggle or who may be even more messed up than we are? The best and most powerful tactic is for us to make a personal commitment to Christ, declare war on terror and get into the fight so we can live in freedom! Ultimately it is a control issue. Satan can control and terrorize you or the love of God can reign in and control our lives and we can be free! Freedom in Christ is a choice. Do you really want to be free? Do you really want to change? Are you tired of Satan controlling your life? Are you willing to fight back and do whatever it takes to be free? If so, then enlist in the Army of God and join the fight for your freedom, for the ones you love and for a new future in Christ!

BATTLE DRILL: Road March Down the "Roman's Road"

How do we enlist in the Army of God and get into the fight? To get into the fight, you don't have to go downtown to your local recruiter to enlist. All you have to do is to take a little walk down the "Roman's Road":

Romans 3:23: For all have sinned and fall short of the glory of God.

Romans 6:23: For the wages of sin is death, but the gift of God is eternal life in Christ Jesus our Lord.

Romans 5:8: But God demonstrates his own love for us in this: While we were still sinners, Christ died for us.

Romans 10:9-10: That if you confess with your mouth, "Jesus is Lord," and believe in your heart that God raised him from the dead, you will be saved. For it is with your heart that you believe and are justified, and it is with your mouth that you confess and are saved.

Romans 10:13: For everyone who calls on the name of the Lord will be saved.

COMMO CHECK:

My prayer: "Dear Lord Jesus, I know that I have sinned and have fallen short many times. I confess my sins to you. I believe you died on the cross for my sins and that you rose from the dead. I give you my heart and my life. Please forgive my sins and take control of my life as my Lord and Savior. Thank you for loving me. Thank you for dying for me. Thank you for forgiving me and for saving me. Thank you for setting me free from my sins and my past. I give you my life, my love and with your help, I will live for you. In Jesus' name, Amen."

Maybe you are already a Christian soldier. You might have enlisted as a child but lately have been AWOL on God. Maybe you are a spiritual combat veteran and have the battle scars to prove it. You might be discouraged by your losses and live in fear of Satan's next roadside bomb or ambush. You may feel like a failure, like quitting and like giving up. I have great news for you! It is time to re-enlist! In Christ, you are never a failure, you are always forgiven and you can be free! Besides, Satan won't quit just because you do, and surrender always brings death.

Surrender is not an option for the Christian. So, it's time for a new determination, a new commitment, and a new faith! "We will not waiver; we will not tire; we will not falter; and we will not fail. Peace and freedom will prevail" (George W. Bush).

1. Have you Enlisted or Reenlisted in the Army of God?

2. Would you like help to know for sure you are a Christian Believer? If so, contact Chaplain David at 850-896-4868 or at armysoldier79@yahoo.com.

MRE: "Are You Lost?"

I once read a front page story in the newspaper about a toddler who had wandered away from home. After about 15 minutes of looking and calling for her three-year-old boy, his frantic mother dialed 911. Sheriff Deputies immediately responded with a search dog and began to comb the area for the lost boy. You can imagine the mother's terror as she thought about the lakes, streams, caves, child predators and dangers the little boy might face on his own. This story has a happy ending as the child was found unharmed at the bottom of a thirty foot ravine not too far from home. The picture of the joyous reunion decorated the newspaper's front page.

In many ways we can be like that child who wandered away from home. We, too, can wander away from the care and protection of our Heavenly Father. In fact, we are spiritually prone to wander. We can become interested in the things of this world and slowly drift away. We can be easily distracted by our busy lives and schedules or we can just decide to leave home and go our own way. I often talk with people whose lives are in a mess and they tell me, "You know, Chaplain, I used to be closed to God" or "I used to be in church every Sunday" or "I just don't pray like I used to."

The problem with spiritual wandering is that without God's loving protection and presence, this world can be a dangerous place as we are constantly in danger of falling prey to Satan's devices.

I have great news for wanderers like us. Our story can also have a happy ending as our loving Heavenly Father keeps on searches and calls for us to come back home to Him. God wants to bring us back into His arms of safety and grace. That is why He sent His Son to the cross in the first place. Just as God went searching for Adam and Eve in the garden when they wandered away, He searches for us when we wander. So, if you find yourself all alone and feeling lost, stop and listen for God's voice and then call out to Him. He will bring you back home into His grace and you can also experience a joyful reunion in the arms of God.

"Then Jesus told them this parable: 'Suppose one of you has a hundred sheep and loses one of them. Does he not leave the ninety-nine in the open country and go after the lost sheep until he finds it? And when he finds it, he joyfully puts it on his shoulders (and goes home). … I tell you that in the same way there will be more rejoicing in heaven over one sinner who repents than over ninety-nine righteous persons who do not need to repent'" (Luke 15:3-5, 7).

Under Attack

On September 11, 2001, millions of Americans watched in horror as almost 3,000 innocent victims lost their lives at the hands of cowardly terrorists. Even though Americans had been targeted by terrorists before, many had never personally experienced such destruction and loss of life watching on live TV right here on American soil. We watched, in horror, as the second plane flew into the tower, as precious souls jumped to their deaths, as the towers fell, and witnessed the terror in the faces of those fleeing from Ground Zero. We will never forget the smoke rising from the Pentagon or the charred grass and wreckage on a Pennsylvania countryside.

On 9-11 the War on Terror truly began for us all. America was forever changed. We realized for the first time how vulnerable we were, how much the enemies of our freedom hated us and wondered when the next attack would come. The War on Terror has also revealed our true character as Americans. We saw the heroism and courage of our firefighters, police officers, the passengers of United Airlines Flight 93 and followed their example as we became determined to "Let's Roll." Millions of Americans turned back to God in prayer and the flag took on a whole new meaning. As a nation, we were angry, determined to fight and confident of future victory and our enduring freedom, at least for a while. Years later, most Americans seem to have forgotten 9-11 and seem unaware that we are a nation still at war, not just in Afghanistan and Iraq, but right here in our own country. Forgetting or ignoring the fact that we are still at war against those who want to kill us and destroy our freedoms doesn't change reality, it only invites disaster.

Even though we may actually remember 9-11 and do realize that we are still a nation at war, we may have forgotten or may have never realized that there is spiritual war and fight for freedom that rages within us all. This spiritual war is just as real and can cause far worse devastation with eternal consequences. Satan is the ultimate terrorist who uses his weapons of "mass destruction" to deceive, terrorize, control, destroy, and to rob us of our freedom in his war against God and all those who are loved by God. Satan knows that he cannot destroy or defeat God, so he hurts God by hurting us.

Most likely, you have experienced your own spiritual 9-11. You have experienced the pain and sorrow of a satanic attack. You bear the battle scars and know first-hand the guilt, frustration, fear, self-hatred, and loss of hope from repeated failure in your struggle for freedom. You may feel like a casualty and consider giving up, but know you don't have a choice. You have to try to fight on, knowing that another attack is inevitable. The spiritual war on terror leaves us with a choice. We can choose to be a victim and suffer in bondage, or we can choose to declare war, fight for our freedom and press on until we achieve the ultimate victory in Christ.

We are not in this war alone. We have each other and most importantly, we have the awesome power and resources of God on our side. The war for eternal freedom has already been won. Jesus Christ has already won the spiritual war on terror through His death on the cross and His resurrection from the dead. You can be different. You can be free. During the next four weeks we will be looking at how, through Christ, we can experience and enjoy our eternal freedom. "The Battle is now joined on many fronts. We will not waiver; we will not tire; we will not falter; and we will not fail. Peace and freedom will prevail. Thank you and God continue to bless America" President Bush (10/7/ 2001).

BATTLE DRILLS:

John 10:7-17

Therefore Jesus said again, "I tell you the truth, I am the gate for the sheep. All who ever came before me were thieves and robbers, but the sheep did not listen to them. I am the gate; whoever enters through me will be saved. He will come in and go out, and find pasture. The thief comes only to steal and kill and destroy; I have come that they may have life, and have it to the full. I am the good shepherd. The good shepherd lays down his life for the sheep. The hired hand is not the shepherd who owns the sheep. So when he sees the wolf coming, he abandons the sheep and runs away. Then the wolf attacks the flock and scatters it. The man runs away because he is a hired hand and cares nothing for the sheep. I am the good shepherd; I know my sheep and my sheep know me--just as the Father knows me and I know the Father--and I lay down my life for the sheep. I have other sheep that are not of this sheep pen. I must bring them also. They too will listen to my voice, and there shall be one flock and one shepherd. The reason my Father loves me is that I lay down my life--only to take it up again."

1 Peter 5:8

Be sober-minded; be watchful. Your adversary the devil prowls around like a roaring lion, seeking someone to devour.

1. **What does this passage say about the devil as a thief, enemy, terrorist?**

2. **What does it mean for me for Jesus to be my Shepherd?**

COMMO CHECK:

Talk to God and thank Him for taking care of you and for giving Jesus to die for your sins. Ask Him to protect you from satanic attack and to help set you free.

My prayer: (Declaration of War) "Lord Jesus, My life has been under attack. I have tried so many times and failed and now I know I need your help. With your help I commit my life to you and declare war on Satan. You died so I could be free and you won the war on the cross. With your help, I can live in freedom and enjoy life. Forgive me for trying to fight this war on my own and give me the strength and courage to stand and to win one day at a time and one battle at a time. I trust you and I believe in you. Thank you for loving me, for dying for me, and for promising to help me. In Jesus' name, Amen."

MRE: "Wounded in Action"

One of the most important missions for a chaplain is caring for our wounded soldiers and their families. Our wounded deserve and get the very best care in the world. Not only do we focus on bringing healing to physical wounds, we also make every effort to help bring healing to the unseen emotional wounds inflicted by combat. These wounds are often far more difficult to treat.

As a chaplain, I have learned that, although we might not have been physically wounded in combat, every one of us has, at some point, been wounded emotionally and spiritually. At times, our wounds are the result of enemy fire (those who want to hurt us), sometimes our wounds are the result of friendly fire (those who are supposed to care about us, but still end up hurting us), sometimes our wounds are simply a result of living in a hostile world, and many times our wounds are self-inflicted (a result of our own poor choices and failures).

How can we find healing when we are wounded in action? While there is some truth in the statement that "time heals all wounds," the very best care for our wounds can be found in the care of the Great Physician. Jesus loves us, died for us and is the only One who can bring complete healing to a broken and wounded heart. He is the only One who can forgive us, help us to forgive others, help us to let go of the past, and give us hope so we can look to the future. His grace is always sufficient to pick us up when we fall down and mend our broken hearts. So, the next time you find yourself cut and bleeding on the inside, take your hurts to the One who can truly make you whole again! Also, be on the lookout for those around you who have also been wounded in action, so you can point them to the loving care of the Great Physician!

Our Battle Plan

Before the Iraq invasion, our battalion's staff spent 12 hours a day for weeks in the desert near the Iraqi border preparing for our first mission once "Operation Iraqi Freedom" kicked off. Our objective had been set and every detail of every eventuality was considered and planned to the very minute. This preparation proved to be effective because once the war began, we moved according to the battle plan and quickly seized our objective. I remembered laughing about how so much time and effort was devoted to the first 24 hours of our assault while during the rest of our time in Iraq, we followed the very basic combat skills which had been a daily part our training even beginning way back in our Basic Training.

Preparation and a good battle plan is also an essential element in spiritual victory. God has provided us with everything we need in order to be victorious against satanic attacks. These weapons and tactics can be found in His Word, the Bible. We will spend the next 4 weeks examining God's battle plan for our freedom. Since the military uses acronyms for everything, we will be using the acronym "FREE" to help us remember four key spiritual principles to bring us freedom. "FREE" stands for:

Faith in Christ

Resist temptation

Experience God

Encourage others

"If the Son sets you free you will be free indeed." The spiritual war on terror and struggle for freedom is fought day by day. Choosing a daily personal commitment of faith in Christ, resisting temptation, experiencing God and encouraging others will ensure we are able to enjoy the freedom we have in Christ. Freedom is not only a dream or a possibility; through Christ, freedom is a promise and can be our reality!

BATTLE DRILLS:

Psalm 118:5: In my anguish I cried to the Lord, and he answered by setting me free.

Psalm 146:5-7: Blessed is he whose help is the God of Jacob, whose hope is in the Lord his God, the Maker of heaven and earth, the sea, and everything in them-- the Lord, who remains faithful forever. He upholds the cause of the oppressed and gives food to the hungry. The Lord sets prisoners free.

Luke 4:18: "The Spirit of the Lord is on me, because he has anointed me to preach good news to the poor. He has sent me to proclaim freedom for the prisoners and recovery of sight for the blind, to release the oppressed ..."

John 8:31-36: Jesus said, "If you hold to my teaching, you are really my disciples. Then you will know the truth, and the truth will set you free." They answered him, we are Abraham's descendants and have never been slaves of anyone. How can you say that we shall be set free? Jesus replied, "I tell you the truth, everyone who sins is a slave to sin. Now a slave has no permanent place in the family, but a son belongs to it forever. So if the Son sets you free, you will be free indeed."

Galatians 5:1: It is for freedom that Christ has set us free. Stand firm, then, and do not let yourselves be burdened again by a yoke of slavery.

Ephesians 3:11-12: according to his eternal purpose which he accomplished in Christ Jesus our Lord. In him and through faith in him we may approach God with freedom and confidence.

1. **How can we be set free and live in freedom?**

2. **Does freedom bring any responsibility on our part? If so, what?**

COMMO CHECK:

Talk to God and thank Him for setting you free and for everything He has done for you in Jesus. Ask Him to help you live in freedom.

My prayer: "Lord Jesus, today I commit my life to live "FREE" in you. Today, I put my *F*aith in you. I believe you love me and I know you are with me. Help me to trust in you totally. Lord, today fill me with your Spirit and help me to *R*esist the devil and temptation and to stay away from anything that might make me fall. Lord Jesus, today help me to *E*xperience you in your Word and to enjoy your presence and peace in my life as I worship you. Finally, Lord Jesus today help me to *E*ncourage someone else who needs your help and your love. I ask this in Jesus' name, Amen."

MRE: "Life Repair"

One Sunday evening as my wife and I were driving to church out in the Tennessee countryside, I noticed a sign in a yard advertising "Computer Repair." This sign caught my attention, as it was hand painted on a white piece of plywood and out in the middle of nowhere. The letters were different sizes and looked if they had been painted by a child. I had to laugh, as I couldn't imagine bringing in my laptop for Bubba to fix. Now, I don't have anything against Bubba. Most of my family from the hills of West Virginia and Kentucky are Bubbas. I love them and even like a few of them, but I wouldn't let them near my laptop. Bubba might be good at fixing cars, building stuff, and fishing, but I will leave my computer repairs to the "computer geeks."

To whom do you turn when your life needs repair? There are times in life when our marriages, family relationships, bodies, emotions, and hearts get broken. When these times come, where do you go? There are a lot of Bubbas out there offering their advice and handiwork. They may advertise on TV, have 900-numbers, possess counseling degrees, or may even be your best friend, but that doesn't mean they really have a clue about how to fix your life. Why not turn to the true Expert in the person of God Himself? God is the one who created life, holds it in His loving hands, who wrote the Book on it, and who always knows how to put it back together whenever it falls apart. So, when you find yourself broken, don't turn to a Bubba. Turn to God and you will never find yourself disappointed!

"Let us therefore come boldly unto the throne of grace that we may obtain mercy, and find grace to help in time of need." (Hebrews 4:16).

ARMY CHAPEL

Got Faith?
(F-Faith)

For three months we waited in the desert of Northern Kuwait. War was inevitable, but so was the outcome. We had no doubt that Saddam's army, even with his prized Republican Guard, were no match for the firepower and might of the United States military. While we were completely confident of the ultimate victory, we wondered about how long the war would last, whether there were weapons of mass destruction, how many of us might become casualties, and we most of all, we worried about our families back home. Eventually I would end my 25 year military career with 4 deployments and almost 3 years in Iraq, Afghanistan, Africa and Kuwait. I don't remember ever doubting the ability of United States to win the War, as long as we were allowed to fight with all we had. For me, the outcome was assured but the day-to-day battles were still yet to be fought. I had faith in the cause of freedom and we were committed to fight and kill terrorists there instead of having to fight them back home.

A little boy once defined faith as, "Hoping for something you know ain't gonna happen." This is a poor definition of faith. Faith is not an irrational leap in the dark or reserved for those who sit in a pew on Sundays. Faith is confidence, assurance, trust, or believing in something or someone you know to be true. Something else about faith; everybody has it. The Christian has faith, but so do the atheist, the agnostic, the doctor, the scientist, the factory worker, the housewife, and even the soldier. Every one of us believes in something or someone. We either have faith in ourselves, in science, in others, in knowing that we can't know, in "something out there," or we can have faith in a personal God who created us, loves us, gave His Son to die for our freedom, and whose power and might will guarantee our ultimate victory in our spiritual war on terror and fight for freedom.

The same God who created the universe loves you! He is all-powerful and undefeated. The forces of Satan are no match against the firepower and might of God and His Army. There is no thing nor person, nor anything else that seeks to control or enslave us that can have any power over us when God is with us and on our side. The spiritual war on terror has already been won. The outcome was sealed when Jesus died on the cross for our sins and rose from the dead for our eternal salvation.

Through faith (trusting and believing) in Jesus and what He has done for us, we receive His forgiveness, His freedom, and real hope and help for the future. So today, stop looking back, looking down or looking within and start looking to Christ in faith. The key that unlocks the chains of addiction and bondage is faith in Christ. "If the Son sets you free, you will be free indeed" (John 8:36).

BATTLE DRILL: Hebrews 11:1-10 & 24-30

Now faith is being sure of what we hope for and certain of what we do not see. This is what the ancients were commended for. By faith we understand that the universe was formed at God's command, so that what is seen was not made out of what was visible. By faith Abel offered God a better sacrifice than Cain did. By faith he was commended as a righteous man, when God spoke well of his offerings. And by faith he still speaks, even though he is dead. By faith Enoch was taken from this life, so that he did not experience death; he could not be found, because God had taken him away. For before he was taken, he was commended as one who pleased God. And without faith it is impossible to please God, because anyone who comes to him must believe that he exists and that he rewards those who earnestly seek him. By faith Noah, when warned about things not yet seen, in holy fear built an ark to save his family. By his faith he condemned the world and became heir of the righteousness that comes by faith. By faith Abraham, when called to go to a place he would later receive as his inheritance, obeyed and went, even though he did not know where he was going. By faith he made his home in the Promised Land like a stranger in a foreign country; he lived in tents, as did Isaac and Jacob, who were heirs with him of the same promise. For he was looking forward to the city with foundations, whose architect and builder is God ... By faith Moses, when he had grown up, refused to be known as the son of Pharaoh's daughter. He chose to be mistreated along with the people of God rather than to enjoy the pleasures of sin for a short time. He regarded disgrace for the sake of Christ as of greater value than the treasures of Egypt, because he was looking ahead to his reward. By faith he left Egypt, not fearing the king's anger; he persevered because he saw him who is invisible. By faith he kept the Passover and the sprinkling of blood, so that the destroyer of the firstborn would not touch the firstborn of Israel. By faith the people passed through the Red Sea as on dry land; but when the Egyptians tried to do so, they were drowned. By faith the walls of Jericho fell, after the people had marched around them for seven days.

By examining this Scripture, describe how faith made a difference in the lives of these Old Testament believers and then how faith can make a difference in your life.

COMMO CHECK:

Ask God to help you grow in faith and to trust Him more. Thank Him for helping you in the past and for all He has done for you and is going to do for you in the future.

MRE: "You're a Winner!"

You might not be able to tell by looking at me, but I am a winner. Years ago, my wife forced me to go with her to an event at a local car dealer where those attending could win a prize. We walked in, received a ticket, endured the sales pitch and waited to see if we would win something. The first fifteen lucky winners received a hat with the dealers name on it, the sixteenth lucky winner won a small stereo system and there we sat with nothing. Imagine our surprise when my number was called and we won a flat-screen television. For once, I was glad I listened to my wife. I didn't even have to do anything. All I had to do was receive my prize. You know, it feels good to be winner!

I am a winner not because I won a TV, I was a winner even before then. In fact, all of us are winners through faith in Christ. Through faith, God has chosen us, adopted us as His own children, forgives our sins, and gave us all the riches of eternal life in heaven. We don't even have to do anything; all we have to do is receive the gift of His love and grace. So today be sure to enjoy God's gifts to you and smile! Why? Because you are a winner in Christ!

"For it is by grace you have been saved, through faith—and this not from yourselves, it is the gift of God—not by works, so that no one can boast" (Ephesians 2:8-9).

ALWAYS ON DUTY

The Soldier the bracelet was one of my Soldiers was killed in Afghanistan.

Army Life
(F-Faith)

From June 2000 through November 2001, I was blessed to serve as the Battalion Chaplain for 1/50th Infantry. The 1/50th was an infantry basic training battalion. As a basic training chaplain, I helped soldiers meet Jesus after they met their drill sergeant. I also helped these new soldiers make the difficult transition from civilian life to Army life. When you raise your right hand and solemnly swear to "support and defend the Constitution of the United States" your life changes. In order to become a soldier, one must be willing to leave family, friends, and the comforts of home behind. Being a soldier means one must be willing to surrender individual rights, to become "Army Strong." To serve as a soldier may mean hardship, sacrifice, difficulty, and the willingness to give your life so others can enjoy the freedoms, you may have to surrender. Combat is no place for wimps, for those who aren't willing to pay the price or for those who joined for the benefits. The commitment to serve your country will definitely and forever change your life.

The commitment to serve Christ and to live in spiritual freedom will change your life even more. To become a Christian you must be willing to leave your past behind. To be a Christian you must be willing to surrender your individual rights and selfish desires to be part of the Army of God. To serve and live as a Christian may mean hardship, sacrifice, difficulty, and being willing to forsake all for the One who gave His life so that we might live and enjoy the freedom which He purchased for us on a cross with His own blood. Combat is not a video game but the bullets, blood and death is for real. Spiritual combat is not just believing in God, being a "good person" or even going to church. Satan is real, hell is real, the blood of Christ was real and so is His love and His power to help us live in spiritual freedom.

So how do we join the Army of God? The requirement is faith which always results in repentance which always results in a changed life. The Biblical word, "repentance," means change. Faith is turning to and trusting in Christ while repentance is turning from sin and self to live for Christ... One reason why so many Christians struggle with sin and spiritual bondage is that they try to live for Christ while not truly letting go of the past and without doing everything possible to make a clean break from sin.

Just as a soldier can't be committed to serve their country and enjoy all the benefits of civilian life at the same time, a Christian can't enjoy freedom in Christ and let themselves continually get tangled up in sinful habits at the same time.

Living in freedom requires a radical separation from sin. A person who struggles with controlling behaviors or controlling people must be willing to totally surrender their heart, mind, attitude, and actions to the control of Christ and the perfecting influence of His Spirit. We must also be willing to separate ourselves from any people or activities that may cause us to fall back into bondage. Just as repentance is a continuous turning from our sin, we must continually be turning to Christ in faith. Faith and repentance are two sides of the same coin. You can't have one without the other. The good news is the grace of God continuity helps us, if we allow Him to, with both faith and repentance.

Living in freedom, requires getting rid of anything or any influence that might cause you to fall back into bondage. Just as you don't play catch with a live hand grenade, you don't play around with sin. Repentance always means radical separation, but the rewards outweigh the cost. Repentance ALWAYS results in forgiveness. Repentance ALWAYS leads to joy. Repentance ALWAYS leads to freedom in Christ! The reality is this, everyone is an addict. We are all addicted to something or someone. There are negative addictions (alcohol, drugs, porn, etc.) and there are positive addictions (for me: grandsons, horses, Christian music and Jesus). Just as we can't turn to Jesus without turning from our sin (faith/repentance), we can't stop a negative addiction without replacing it with a positive addiction and the best positive addiction is Jesus and His love. That is what it takes to live for Christ in freedom.

BATTLE DRILLS:

2 Timothy 2:1-4: You then, my son, be strong in the grace that is in Christ Jesus. And the things you have heard me say in the presence of many witnesses entrust to reliable men who will also be qualified to teach others. Endure hardship with us like a good soldier of Christ Jesus. No one serving as a soldier gets involved in civilian affairs--he wants to please his commanding officer.

Matthew 4:17: ... Repent for the Kingdom of Heaven is at hand.

Mark 1:15: The time has come, he said, the kingdom of God is near. Repent and believe the good news!

Luke 13:3: But unless you repent, you too will all perish.

Acts 3:19: Repent, then, and turn to God, so that your sins may be wiped out, that times of refreshing may come from the Lord.

What are some things in my life that I need to quit, get rid of or to let go and give them to Jesus in faith?

What are some things I need to start doing to help take the place of the negative in my life?

COMMO CHECK:

Talk to God and ask Him to forgive your past and to help you forgive yourself to let go of the past. Ask God to help change you into what He wants you to be. Thank Him for loving you and for His forgiveness and His grace.

MRE: "3X Clean"

Those who know me know that I am a little off which explains a lot. If you need any more proof, here it is. Recently my wife bought a new brand of soap which had this guarantee in large print on the front of the bottle, "3X Clean Guaranteed!" As soon as I read this bold proclamation I wondered, "How would you know? What if you were only as clean or what if you are only twice as clean?" I then turned the bottle over and read the small print which stated, "If you are not completely satisfied with this product you can mail your receipt to the following address..." I then wondered who would save their commissary receipt and wait several weeks for a $1.49 refund check if they were not clean enough. I guess instead of going through all that trouble, I will just have to be satisfied with being as clean or maybe twice as clean.

I am thankful that when we feel dirty spiritually, due to our sin and guilt, we can always find complete cleansing in God's grace and in the arms of Jesus. While there is nothing we can do to cleanse ourselves, we can be made totally pure in Christ. How? The answer is found in 1 John 1:9, "If we confess our sins, He is faithful and just and will forgive us our sins, and purify us from all unrighteousness." So, feeling dirty? Come to God for a cleansing that is completely guaranteed!

"'Come now, let us reason together,' says the Lord. 'Though your sins are like scarlet, they shall be as white as snow; though they are red as crimson, they shall be like wool'" (Isaiah 1:18).

R&R
Rewind & Review

Review Questions:

1. In the story of the Prodigal Son, contrast the Prodigal's search for freedom and what he found and compare how he found true freedom:

2. In what ways can Satan be described as the "ultimate terrorist?"

3. What does the "Romans Road" say about our Sin? God's Love? Salvation?

4. **What is the relationship between Faith, Grace and Good Works in Ephesians 2:8-10?**

MRE: "Who is Flying this Thing?"

As a deployed Chaplain, I have traveled many places via convoys, route clearance and with PSDs (Personal Security Details). I have also flown thousands of miles via C17, C5, C130 as well as Blackhawk and Chinook helicopters. I noticed something about all my flights; at no point did the pilot ask for my help or advice about how to fly the aircraft. Why not? Did the pilots know that even though I had flown many times that I wasn't a pilot and that I had no clue about how to fly a helicopter or airplane? Did they know that I had no idea how to get where we were going? Do you think they had made this trip numerous times before and knew they didn't need my help? The good news for all of us was that all our aviators were fully qualified and capable and did in fact get us safely to our destination, without any help, advice, guidance or assistance from me.

While it may seem silly, foolish or even crazy for someone who had never flown before to try to fly a helicopter or airplane all by themselves, we do it all the time in life. Instead of trusting in God to guide us and carry us through life, we often take control of our lives and take the lives of our loved ones into our own hands. Even though God wrote "the Book" (Bible) on how to live, on how to be happy, on how to have a good marriage, on how to raise a family, on how to have a meaningful life, and even more important, on how to make it to heaven, somehow we think we can do better than the God who created and who runs the universe. Even though God is omniscient, we somehow think we are smarter and know more about our lives than He does. Even though God is omnipotent, we think we can do better. Even though God is omnipresent, we are afraid of being alone and even though God loves us enough to give His own Son for us, we don't trust Him to take care of us and provide for all our needs. It all really comes down to this, we just like to be in control and think that we know what we are doing when we really aren't and we really don't. This is why so many lives and homes crash and burn and why so many lives are devastated and left in shambles.

Take it from a chaplain who has seen it and learned it over and over again (and is still learning it), the ONLY way for us to be truly happy, successful and make it safely to our heavenly home, is for us to surrender the control of our lives to God. By the way, He isn't interested in being your "co-pilot" either. God knows what He is doing, loves you a billion times more than anyone else loves you, knows where He is going, and He is the only way for you to find true joy, peace, happiness, love, meaning, and eternal life. So when it comes to your life and your eternal life, let God be the Lord of your life. To do otherwise would be just silly, foolish, or even crazy. If you do, I promise you that your trip will go far more smoothly and you are even guaranteed to make it safely home to your final destination (heaven)!

"The Lord delights in those who fear Him, who put their hope in His unfailing love" (Psalm 147:11).

**COL. DAVID K. TROGDON, CHAPLAIN BETWEEN TWO
SERVICEMEN READY FOR BATTLE.**

Why Are We Here?
(F-Faith)

In July 2002 my chaplain's assistant and I had the opportunity to go to Africa and to meet General Tommy Franks. Our meeting didn't go as I would've hoped. General Franks came to visit our remote (very, very remote) base that was involved in anti-terrorist operations. During his pep talk he asked the question, "Why are we here?" When we didn't answer he asked again, "Why are we here?" Again no one said a word. Suddenly he looked all the way across the DFAC (dining facility) and yelled, "I'll tell you what, Rock of the Marne, and if you don't know why we are here I'm going to tell you!" My heart immediately skipped a few beats, as my assistant and I were the only two soldiers in the room wearing 3rd ID patches. He walked over to our table and looked my young PFC in the eyes and said, "We are here because on 9-11 terrorists killed 3,000 Americans and we are here to kill terrorists!" My shocked, wide-eyed assistant could only nod in agreement and he never recovered from his "conversation" with a 4-star general. I continued to ask him every now and then, "Why are we here?" If soldiers are going to sacrifice, fight, and maybe even die, it is vital that they have a clear understanding of the reason for their service. Soldiers must never forget why we are here.

What about you? Why are you here? What is your purpose in life? Is life about having a good time, the next promotion, finding the perfect hot girl or guy, making money, buying new toys, or is there something and someone far more important? Life is not about us getting what we want or doing whatever we want. Life is about Jesus!

As a Christian soldier, life is about pleasing and fulfilling the mission of our Commander-in-Chief. Jesus died on the cross so that our sins could be forgiven and we could be free and live in freedom. Through faith in Christ, our sins are totally forgiven and we are free. We don't have to live in fear or in bondage to anyone or anything! We can say "NO" to temptation and to anything or anyone that might rob us of the life Jesus died for us to have. We are free, not only to enjoy our freedom but to help others find their freedom in Christ.

Life is not about you or me. Life is about Christ! Faith is not just believing that Jesus is a real person. Faith is about living for Christ! Faith is not just about receiving forgiveness. True faith always results in love for God and a life of faithfulness to God! Faithfulness means living to please God, our Commander-in-Chief. Faith is about obedience to His orders for life.

Any controlling or enslaving attitude or behavior, is ultimately a method of satanic control and a form of idolatry. We worship whoever or whatever is in control of our lives. We are worshipping an idol anytime we allow someone or something else, other than God to be the center of our affection, attention or to have control. Sin takes away not only our freedom but also cause us to lose our focus on our true purpose in life, which is living for Christ. When you are tempted to give in to temptation, just remember why you are here.

BATTLE DRILL:

Philippians 1:21a: For me, to live is Christ....

Romans 12:1-2: Therefore, I urge you, brothers, in view of God's mercy, to offer your bodies as living sacrifices, holy and pleasing to God--this is your spiritual act of worship. Do not conform any longer to the pattern of this world, but be transformed by the renewing of your mind. Then you will be able to test and approve what God's will is--his good, pleasing and perfect will.

Galatians 2:19-20: For through the law I died to the law so that I might live for God. I have been crucified with Christ and I no longer live, but Christ lives in me. The life I live in the body, I live by faith in the Son of God, who loved me and gave himself for me.

1. **According to these Scriptures, why am I here? What is God's purpose for my life?**

2. What does it mean for me to live for Christ?

COMMO CHECK:

Thank Jesus for dying for you on the cross and ask Him to help you live for Him every day.

MRE: "God's VIP"

Back in May of 2004, I was preparing for the arrival of a VIP. No, it wasn't the President, senator, congressman or General Tommy Franks, but someone far more important. I was preparing for the arrival of my first of now four grandsons, Nathaniel. In order to get ready for the arrival of my VIP, I worked on my "Papa's SOP." Here is an excerpt:

1. Hold him all the time.

2. If crying, insert pacifier.

3. If pacifier fails, insert bottle.

4. If bottle fails and something smells, call NayNay.

5. Remember these three words, "Want a toy?"

Being a grandparent is so much fun! I never realized how much I could love my grandsons. They are truly are truly VIPs to me. I enjoy spending all the time I can spoiling Papa's boys.

I have some great news for you. You are God's VIP. You could never imagine how much He loves you! He will hold you when you are crying, feed you when you are hungry and clean you up when you get dirty. He loves to pour out His blessings on His children. So, anytime the circumstances of life leave you feeling unimportant or even unwanted, remember that to your Heavenly Father you are His precious VIP!

"For he chose us in him before the creation of the world to be holy and blameless in his sight. In love, he predestined us to be adopted as his sons through Jesus Christ, in accordance with his pleasure and will" (Ephesians 1:4-5).

David K. Trogdon, Chaplain (LTC), USA, Ret.

The War is already Won

(F-Faith)

We were all lined up with somewhere to go. Finally, after three months of waiting in the desert of Northern Kuwait, the 3rd Infantry Division was sitting on the border waiting for the order "GO!" We had arrived at the border earlier in the day and grew more excited every time we looked across into Iraq. The butterflies grew when we received orders to put on our J-List Chemical garments. We knew that the time was near. At about 2000 (8:00 p.m.), our artillery opened up to take out the Iraqi border posts. It was then that we knew for certain that the invasion of Iraq was on. As we crossed the border, our adrenaline was high, but so was our motivation. We were told the faster we got to Baghdad, the faster we would go home.

As the war began, there was so much we didn't know. Would the Iraqis fight? Would Saddam use his WMDs? Were our families okay? When would we see home again? While there was much we didn't know, there was one thing that was certain -- the outcome. We knew beyond a shadow of a doubt that we would win. There was no way Saddam, even with his Republican Guard, could stand against the power and might of the U.S. military. The outcome was sure; the only question was how long it would take and how many lives would be lost. If you have to go to war, you do feel much better knowing that you cannot lose and that victory is sure.

The war for spiritual freedom has already been won. When Jesus died on the cross, He paid for all our sins; past, present and future. Satan used every weapon in his arsenal to keep Jesus from dying on the cross and then, in desperation, to keep Jesus in the tomb. When Jesus arose victoriously, Satan's defeat was complete. Through faith in Christ we are winners. Our sins are gone and our future is bright. Jesus won the war for us and all we have to do is fight the day-to-day battles. Not only has the war already been won, Satan's power and weapons are no match for the power and might of God.

The spiritual "reality" proclaims that because of Jesus you are a winner. You are forgiven! You have been adopted into the family of God and you are free. Because of the cross we don't have to live in failure.

We don't have to be in bondage and we don't have to give in to temptation. We can say "NO!" to sin and "YES!" to God. We can live and enjoy life in Christ. Not only are we free from our past, we can live free in the future. We already are free. Satan is losing and desperate.

In Christ, the outcome is certain. The war has already been won. It is only a matter of time and how many more battles we have yet to fight. So enjoy the freedom and face the future with confidence. While we know the outcome of our spiritual war on terror, there are still a number of questions. When and how will Satan attack next? How will I respond? How long am I going to keep on struggling? What can I do to better protect myself and be ready for his attacks? Hopefully, many of questions will be answered during the next few weeks as we continue our study. Ultimately, all of these questions will be answered day-by-day as we fight in our spiritual war.

BATTLE DRILLS: Joshua 1:1-9

After the death of Moses the servant of the Lord, the Lord said to Joshua son of Nun, Moses' aide: "Moses my servant is dead. Now then, you and all these people, get ready to cross the Jordan River into the land I am about to give to them--to the Israelites. I will give you every place where you set your foot, as I promised Moses. Your territory will extend from the desert to Lebanon, and from the great river, the Euphrates--all the Hittite country--to the Great Sea on the west. No one will be able to stand up against you all the days of your life. As I was with Moses, so I will be with you; I will never leave you nor forsake you. Be strong and courageous, because you will lead these people to inherit the land I swore to their forefathers to give them. Be strong and very courageous. Be careful to obey all the law my servant Moses gave you; do not turn from it to the right or to the left, that you may be successful wherever you go. Do not let this Book of the Law depart from your mouth; meditate on it day and night, so that you may be careful to do everything written in it. Then you will be prosperous and successful. Have I not commanded you? Be strong and courageous. Do not be terrified; do not be discouraged, for the Lord your God will be with you wherever you go."

1. **What promises do we see in this passage?**

2. **What are our responsibilities in this passage?**

COMMO CHECK:

Talk to God and thank Him for always being with you and His promise of complete freedom and victory in your life. Ask Him to help you be faithful to love Him and to help you live for Him.

MRE: God in Iraq

Where can I go from your spirit? Where can I flee from your presence? If I go up to the heavens, you are there; if I make my bed in the depths, you are there" (Psalm 139:7-8).

After almost 3 years and 4 deployments, I can tell you with certainty that God is definitely in Kuwait, Africa, Iraq and Afghanistan. I know He is always with me because I have seen Him many times. Before you worry that this chaplain is indeed crazy, well I am. Let me explain. I have personally seen God repeatedly in how He has miraculously protected me and my Soldiers, Airmen, Sailors and Marines. I have been run over, surrounded, ambushed, shot at, and rocketed on many occasions, but here I am still here enjoying the blessings of God and the ministry He has provided for me.

I have experienced the sorrow and heartbreak of losing way too many of America's best men and women but I have also often been amazed how God miraculously protected so many others who could have been killed, including myself. My heart often skipped a beat as I received reports about they have hit IEDs or been in firefights only to hear that they were totally unharmed. Even many of those who were wounded, could have been hurt much worse or even killed. This always provides me with an opportunity to point them to God's love and protection in their lives. I know that I am alive today and so many of my Soldiers are alive today because God was with us and was watching over us. Now that I am an old, crusty veteran, I can still say that God is still with me and He is with you too, even in Florida and even when you can't see Him or feel His presence.

(EOD PSALM) "Keep me, O LORD, from the hands of the wicked who plan to trip my feet. Proud men have hidden a snare for me; they have spread out the cords of their net and have set traps for me along my path" (Psalm 140:4-5).

Winning by Losing
(F-Faith)

Sometimes the only way to win is to lose. One of the missions of combat engineers is to secure and control EPWs (Enemy Prisoners of War). While visiting our Bravo Company outside of Karbala, I had the opportunity to see a number of EPWs. Many had willingly surrendered after offering little resistance. Some of the EPWs were released but kept coming back for food and safety. They were fed, received medical treatment and were protected. Many were only fighting because they had been forced to fight. One EPW said, through an interpreter, "The Fedeyean came into my house and killed half of my family. They told me if we didn't fight the Americans they would kill the rest of my family. I decided to take my chances and protect my family by fighting the Americans. I was glad to surrender. My family is safe and I am alive." These Iraqi "volunteers" found freedom only after they surrendered.

Spiritually, the only way to win is to lose. Without Christ we face the terror and control of an evil dictator in Satan. We are unable to resist him or set ourselves free by fighting on our own. Life without Christ always leaves us empty, hurting, helpless, and hopeless. The key to winning is for us to recognize our need for His help, surrender to Jesus, allow Him to set us free, and then everyday ask Him to help us live in freedom.

The Apostle Paul says, "I can do all things through Christ who strengthens me." This means that with Christ's help we can live in and enjoy freedom. We can say "NO!" and resist the urge (temptation) to give in. We can enjoy life. Our lives truly can be different and we can change.

The opposite is also true; without Christ we can do nothing. Without surrendering to Christ and without His help we are doomed to failure. Without Christ's help, we try to fight on our own and we will always be outgunned and out measured. No amount of self-determination, willpower or self-help will be enough to break the power of the things, circumstances and substances that keep us in bondage. If we could quit or change on our own, no one would ever live in bondage. If we had the power to change on our own we would. It is not just enough to stop doing something if we still live in fear and don't have joy for living.

Jesus is our key to true freedom. Jesus not only delivers us, He sets us free!

Faith is trusting in Christ, moment by moment, to help us live in the freedom. He has purchased for us with his blood. Faith provides us with a choice: we can live as a slave under a cruel dictator or we can surrender to Christ and ask for his help. Jesus is the only way to freedom and the only source of all we need for life.

BATTLE DRILL:

Romans 12:1-2: Therefore, I urge you, brothers, in view of God's mercy, to offer your bodies as living sacrifices, holy and pleasing to God--this is your spiritual act of worship. Do not conform any longer to the pattern of this world, but be transformed by the renewing of your mind. Then you will be able to test and approve what God's will is--his good, pleasing and perfect will.

Philippians 3:7-8: But whatever was to my profit I now consider loss for the sake of Christ. What is more, I consider everything a loss compared to the surpassing greatness of knowing Christ Jesus my Lord, for whose sake I have lost all things. I consider them rubbish that I may gain Christ ...

1. **What does it mean for us to offer our bodies as "living sacrifices to God?**

2. **What are some things I need to "lose" so I can "gain" a better knowledge of Christ?**

COMMO CHECK:

Talk to God and surrender total control of your life to Him. Ask Him to give you strength and help in order to live for Him.

MRE: "Rescue at Mile Marker 18"

One day, while stationed at Ft. Campbell, KY, we were on our way back from Nashville on I-24 West, I noticed something small right at mile marker 18. The volume of traffic was heavy and moving at about 75 mph when I noticed a little black kitten standing right next to the interstate watching the cars and tracker trailers fly by. Now because I am a "manly man," I am not a cat guy. I love dogs, but I do have to admit that I have a soft spot in my heart for little kittens. I mentioned my kitty sighting to my wife which led to the following conversion:

David, go back and get it! What? We have to go back and help that kitten. Honey, the next exit is 7 miles up ahead. What are the chances that by the time we go to exit 11, turn around, go back to exit 19 and turn around, that this kitten will still be alive and that we will be able to find it again? Well, we have to try. Okay honey, but I will want a reward from you (anytime I can get a kiss from the hot blonde babe I am going for it!).

With my reward in mind, we went back in search of this little lost kitten. To my amazement, right there, still standing at mile marker 18, still trying to cross the busy interstate, stood the confused kitty. We pulled over, turned on our emergency flashers and walked back to our kitten in distress. Our hearts kept skipping a beat as the kitten would run out into the traffic only to run back to the shoulder of the highway just a half second before being crushed the wheels of a speeding tractor trailer. I walked up to the kitten, which appeared to be about 6-8 weeks old, and the kitten took a defensive position and hissed at me. I picked her up and we carried her away from the danger and certain death to safety. As soon as we were in my truck, this kitty immediately took up with my wife.

Since I know that little kittens, which I like, grow up to be cats, which I don't like, and I know that my dog wouldn't enjoy a feline housemate, I knew we had to come up with a different plan for our new kitten. We decided to take this newly saved kitten to an 11-year-old girl, named Leah, who needed a friend. I wish you could have seen the joy on Leah's face as we introduced her to her new friend. The kitten was named "Clare" because Leah was practicing the clarinet when we pulled up. Hopefully, Clare will live happily ever after in a world free of speeding cars and tractor-trailers.

We may not realize it, but we have much in common with Clare. Here are some spiritual lessons for us from the rescue at mile marker 18:

1.　　Many of us have been rejected and pushed out on our own. All of us have been lost and some of us still may be lost without Christ.

2.　　Without Christ, all of us are helpless, hopeless and in great danger.

3.　　Even though everyone else may pass us by, Jesus always cares for us.

4.　　Our Lord always takes the time to help us, even though it did cost Him the ultimate sacrifice on the cross to save us.

5.　　We often resist God's help because of our sinful pride.

6.　　Jesus wants to carry us to safety and care for all our needs.

7.　　We can live happily ever after when we are introduced to our new Friend in Christ who loves us and cares for us.

So today if you have never been rescued, you too are in danger, but don't worry, you do have a Friend in Jesus! "For the Son of Man came to seek and to save what was lost" (Luke 19:10).

Guard Duty

(R-Resist)

Do you remember your 1ˢᵗ General Order? I sure do. I learned it way back in February of 1979 while attending Basic Training at Ft. Dix, NJ. By the way, I also remember my Drill Sergeants by name. The 1ˢᵗ General Order states, "I will guard everything within the limits of my post and quit my post only when properly relieved." A few nights later, I found my 17 year old self up in a guard tower with my M16A1 rile, with no ammo, guarding something which I didn't even know what I was guarding. In 1981, while at Ft. Bragg, I found my 19 year old self this time guarding warehouses at night with a sawed off baseball bat. I remember wondering how my "weapon" would fare against robbers with real weapons. Years later, guard duty and security would play a much more vital role in places like Iraq and Afghanistan where being on guard against the enemy was truly a matter of life and death. During these times, my "weapon" was faith in God as I prayed and relied upon His protection for all of us as well as relying on my Chaplain's Assistant and my fellow Soldiers to help provide security for an unarmed chaplain.

Guard duty and security is also a vital element in the spiritual war on Terror. It is not a question of if Satan will attack, but only how, when and where. Satan, like any terrorist, likes to hit us when we are not paying attention, when we are vulnerable and definitely by exporting our weaknesses.

Spiritual security begins with guarding and "securing the borders" of our minds and hearts. We must be on guard against allowing evil influences and bad attitudes to slip into our minds undetected or unchecked. We must allow the Holy Spirit to guard our minds by controlling what we think about, what we look at, what or who we listen to, what we indulge in, and especially what or who we touch. Satan is looking for a weakness in our defenses so he can get his foot in the door.

Our modern era of television, social media, the Internet, sexual immorality, lack of moral absolutes (right or wrong) mixed in with a "if it feels good, do it" mentality, provides fertile ground for Satan and his forces to carry out terrorist plots, to rob us of our joy and freedom and ultimately to destroy our lives. We must close our borders against any and all sinful and unholy influences. How? WWJD! Make these four letters into far more than bumper sticker religion by living by What Would Jesus Do? What would Jesus be pleased with me doing? In other words if we wouldn't watch it, do it, think it, say it, taste it, touch it, listen to it, or try it in front of Jesus Himself, then don't do it! Remember He is ALWAYS with us so whatever we do, we do or say or think it in front of Him. Sin begins in the mind. If we don't allow temptation in, then sin won't come out.

Even as we are securing the borders of our mind, we must also allow our hearts to be "secured" by the Holy Spirit. You can't board an airplane without having your bag x-rayed or without passing through a metal detector. We must allow God to screen our hearts constantly for dangerous influences. When the Bible speaks of "guarding our heart" it is not talking about that blood-pumping organ in our chest, but our values, loves, motives, and priorities. Our heart is the center of our emotions, personalities and desires. We love with our hearts and we live by following our hearts, so guard your heart!

BATTLE DRILLS:

Psalm 139:23-24: Search me, O God, and know my heart; test me and know my anxious thoughts. See if there is any offensive way in me, and lead me in the way everlasting.

1 Corinthians 16:13-14: Be on your guard; stand firm in the faith; be men of courage; be strong. Do everything in love.

Philippians 4:4-9: Rejoice in the Lord always. I will say it again: Rejoice! Let your gentleness be evident to all. The Lord is near. Do not be anxious about anything, but in everything, by prayer and petition, with thanksgiving, present your requests to God. And the peace of God, which transcends all understanding, will guard your hearts and your minds in Christ Jesus. Finally, brothers, whatever is true, whatever is noble, whatever is right, whatever is pure, whatever is lovely, whatever is admirable--if anything is excellent or praiseworthy--think about such things. Whatever you have learned or received or heard from me, or seen in me--put it into practice. And the God of peace will be with you.

Colossians 3:1-2: Since, then, you have been raised with Christ, set your hearts on things above, where Christ is seated at the right hand of God. Set your minds on things above, not on earthly things.

1. **How can God help you guard your heart and mind?**

2. **What are some things we should do to be on guard in our hearts and minds?**

COMMO CHECK:

Talk to God and ask for Him to help you be aware of and stay away from any bad influence and to resist temptation. Ask Him to help guard your heart and mind and to be pure sinful thoughts and actions.

MRE: "What If I fail?"

One of the greatest tests of character is how we handle failure. While success may go to our heads, failure can go to our heads and break our hearts and wills. Failure is a part of life and always leaves us facing a choice. We can give up and quit, or we can get up and keep going. I have read that Thomas Edison failed more than 2,000 times in his attempt to help us flip on a light switch. If he had given up after one try or 100 tries or 1,000 tries or even after 1,999 tries, we might still be sitting in the dark today.

In the eyes of God, a failure is not one tries and does not succeed, but one fails to trust in Him to make them a success through faith in Christ. I have good news for you today. God only uses failures! All of us have failed and keep on failing short, but God still uses us in spite of this. Remember the examples of Abraham (lied), Moses (killed a man in anger), Rahab (was once a harlot), Samson (got in trouble trying to be a ladies' man), David (committed adultery and murder), Thomas (struggled with doubt), Peter (often spoke without thinking and denied he even knew Jesus three times), and the Apostle Paul (once was a persecutor). God was able to change and use each one of these heroes of the faith to do great things. If he can change and use them, he can change and use you! So, today if you are feeling like a failure, welcome to the club! Remember the Word of God when He speaks to the Apostle Paul in Corinthians.

"To keep me from becoming conceited because of these surpassingly great revelations, there was given me a thorn in my flesh, a messenger of Satan, to torment me. Three times I pleaded with the Lord to take it away from me. But he said to me, "My grace is sufficient for you, for my power is made perfect in weakness." Therefore I will boast all the more gladly about my weaknesses, so that Christ's power may rest on me. That is why, for Christ's sake, I delight in weaknesses, in insults, in hardships, in persecutions, in difficulties. For when I am weak, then I am strong" (2 Corinthians 12:7-10).

Results: Know Your Enemy (Part 1)
(R-Resist)

Good military intelligence, though some see it as a contradiction in turns, is an essential element in any war effort. Knowing your enemy is a vital part of a successful battle plan. Before the Iraq invasion, we knew the basic locations and conditions of Saddam's conventional forces. We believed we knew his capabilities and knew that he had previously possessed and used WMDs. We didn't know, whether his soldiers would fight, or if he still had or would use WMDs against us. We also didn't know the effectiveness of our training and equipment if Saddam did use WMD's against our forces. While the U.S. has, by far, the very best intelligence gathering capabilities in the world, warfare is often challenged by uncertainties. Good intelligence requires collecting, analyzing, and some assumptions. Often previous actions are some of the best indications of future strategies and plans.

In our spiritual war on terror we have the very best intelligence possible in the Word of God. The Bible is God's "intelligence summary." God gave us the Scriptures so we might come to know Jesus as our personal Lord and Savior, but also that we might know the tactics, plans and strategies of our enemy, the devil. While we cannot predict exactly when and where he will attack next, we can know how to protect ourselves from being his next victim.

The Bible tells us that Satan was once the most beautiful of the angels in the service of God until his pride led to his fall. In an effort to actually take the place of God and receive worship, Satan led a rebellion of a third of all the angels against God. While Satan is powerful, he is not omnipotent (all-powerful), omniscient (all-knowing) or omnipresent. Satan and his angels (demons) lost in their war against God and were cast out of Heaven and are now facing their future eternal punishment in hell.

You may be wondering, "What does rebellion in Heaven have to do with me here and now?" The answer is simple: Satan is like a suicide bomber and wants to cause destruction and pain and take as many with him as he can. He also knows that he is no match for God's power and, like every terrorist, would rather attack the unsuspecting, the weak and the helpless.

Why? Satan knows that the best way to hurt God is to hurt the ones whom God loves so dearly.

Not only is Satan out to destroy the ones that God loves, Satan hasn't changed. He still wants so badly to be worshipped and served in the place of God. Every time we give into temptation or every time we "do our own thing" and act contrary to God's will, we ultimately are serving and worshiping the devil. Satan wants us to serve him and be in control of our lives and will use every weapon in his arsenal to do just that. Every sin is addictive, and a life controlled by sin will always bring bondage, pain, destruction and much happiness to the devil's heart. Just as Satan hoped to take the place of God in Heaven he hopes to take God's place in our hearts. Jesus made it very clear. We either are serving God or we are serving an evil dictator in the devil. The choice then becomes ours, "Which side are we on?" May we be like Joshua and say "As for me and my household we will serve the Lord!" (Joshua 24:15).

BATTLE DRILLS:

Isaiah 14:12-15: How you have fallen from heaven, O morning star, son of the dawn! You have been cast down to the earth, you who once laid low the nations! You said in your heart, "I will ascend to heaven; I will raise my throne above the stars of God; I will sit enthroned on the mount of assembly, on the utmost heights of the sacred mountain. I will ascend above the tops of the clouds; I will make myself like the Most High. But you were brought down to the grave, to the depths of the pit."

Revelation 12:9-11: The great dragon was hurled down--that ancient serpent called the devil, or Satan, who leads the whole world astray. He was hurled to the earth, and his angels with him... the accuser of our brothers, who accuses them before our God day and night, has been hurled down. They overcame him by the blood of the Lamb and by the word of their testimony...

1 Peter 5:8-9: Be self-controlled and alert. Your enemy the devil prowls around like a roaring lion looking for someone to devour. Resist him, standing firm in the faith...

1. What do these Scriptures teach us about what the devil wants to do in your life?

2. What do these Scriptures teach us about how we can resist the Devil?

COMMO CHECK:

Talk to God and ask Him to help you resist satanic temptations and to stay away from his traps. Thank Him for His grace and power to live in freedom.

MRE: "Beware of the Skunk?"

Once I was late leaving the hospital at Ft. Campbell when I noticed a cat on the sidewalk about 50 feet ahead. Immediately something inside of me knew something wasn't right. This cat walked a little funny and had a big bushy tail. It was then that I realized that this was not your ordinary house cat. This cat was a skunk! At that moment I knew I had a decision to make. I could keep walking and try to ignore the skunk hoping he or she would ignore me. I could go up and try to make friends with the skunk by offering food and petting its tail. I could invite the skunk home with me and introduce him or her to my wife as our new adopted pet or I could have done what I knew was the best option.

I froze in my tracks, waited for the skunk to move out of sight and then took a different path to my truck. The good news is that due to my wise choice of action that both the skunk and I went our separate ways, both smelling as good, or as bad, as we did before our encounter.

While God loves all of His creation, some of us stink more than others and need to be avoided for our own good. God loves us all (John 3:16). All of us stink a little from time to time (Romans 3:23), but a few, for our own good, need to be avoided until God cleanses them (1 John 1:9). We warn our children about the dangers of following the crowd and bad influences. We remind them concerning the need to choose friends wisely. We have also watched with broken hearts as marriages were torn apart by "harmless" friendships with another woman or another man.

Don't you wish dangerous relationships were as easy to spot as a skunk? The key to spotting a "trouble" is to walk carefully and listen to the voice of God's Spirit as He speaks to your heart and through His Word. Also, the best thing to do when you encounter "trouble" is not to befriend him or her, feed them or marry them, but to stop, pray and go another way. Doing so will save your life and your home from a lot of stink.

Results: Know Your Enemy (Part 2)

(R-Resist)

Once we arrived in Kuwait, and especially after the invasion, we were constantly reminded to "make ourselves a hard target." This exhortation was in recognition of some of the basic terrorist tactics. Terrorists rarely attack prepared and heavily armed forces in a frontal assault. Terrorists prefer ambushes, IEDs, car bombs and RPGs. Terrorists seek out the weak and unarmed or hide behind women and children and love to hit and run. Terrorists hope to control through fear and intimidation and to use the power of the media to demoralize those who seek to live in freedom. Terrorists know that even though they cannot win a conventional war; they can achieve much by wearing down our will to fight and inflict as many casualties as possible. The terrorist wins every time we show our weakness and a lack of commitment to the fight for freedom.

Satanic terrorism has much in common with terrorism around the world today. Satan and his forces are always looking to exploit our weaknesses and vulnerabilities. Satanic temptation is so effective and sin so addictive because it always looks good, feels good and fools us into thinking it that it is right, okay, good for us, what we really deserve or at least what we want.

Satan is smart enough to disguise his "IEDs" in nice little harmless-looking packages. Adultery can begin with a pretty smile or a compliment. Alcoholism and drug addiction flourishes in our need to feel better or relax a little. Materialism and the love of money rule us in our desire to get ahead, have nice things and be happy.

Even though sin may at first look good, taste good and makes us feel good, these effects are only temporary. Sin quickly turns ugly, leaves a sour taste and leaves us feeling guilty, dirty, ashamed, and empty. Satan realizes that we have an empty place in our heart that only a right relationship with God can completely fill. He also realizes that we all are searching for fulfillment so he provides plenty of cheap, easy, but deadly, substitutes to the love of God.

The best way to prevent becoming a victim or casualty due to a satanic attack is for us to be a "hard target." Draw close to Christ and allow his love and presence to completely satisfy that "God-shaped void" which is in every life. The love of Christ is always beautiful, always enjoyable and always completely satisfying. So when temptation comes, say "NO" to the devil and "YES" to Christ!

BATTLE DRILLS:

James 4:7-8: Submit yourselves, then, to God. Resist the devil, and he will flee from you. Come near to God and he will come near to you.

1 Corinthians 10:12-13: So, if you think you are standing firm, be careful that you don't fall! No temptation has seized you except what is common to man. And God is faithful; he will not let you be tempted beyond what you can bear. But when you are tempted, he will also provide a way out so that you can stand up under it.

Matthew 4:1-11: Then Jesus was led by the Spirit into the desert to be tempted by the devil. After fasting forty days and forty nights, he was hungry. The tempter came to him and said, "If you are the Son of God, tell these stones to become bread." Jesus answered, "It is written: 'Man does not live on bread alone, but on every word that comes from the mouth of God.'" Then the devil took him to the holy city and had him stand on the highest point of the temple. "If you are the Son of God," he said, "throw yourself down. For it is written: 'He will command his angels concerning you, and they will lift you up in their hands, so that you will not strike your foot against a stone.'" Jesus answered him, "It is also written: 'Do not put the Lord your God to the test.'" Again, the devil took him to a very high mountain and showed him all the kingdoms of the world and their splendor. "All this I will give you," he said, "if you will bow down and worship me." Jesus said to him, "Away from me, Satan! For it is written: 'Worship the Lord your God, and serve him only.'" Then the devil left him, and angels came and attended him.

1. What do these Scriptures teach us about how to resist the devil when he attacks?

2. What are some satanic IEDs Satan tries to us against you?

COMMO CHECK:

Talk to God and ask Him to help you to draw close to Jesus and to help you stand firm and to resist the devil's tricks and influences in your life.

MRE: "Don't Harass the Alligators?"

"NO SWIMMING. DO NOT FEED OR HARASS THE ALLIGATORS." Really? We actually needed signs posted around the two ponds on our 4th Infantry Brigade Vanguard Complex warning us against swimming, feeding or even harassing our alligators? The answer is quite simply, YES! The Army always does manage to have a few select Soldiers who seem to lack the common sense necessary to know that alligators are not puppies. I had been a chaplain and Soldier long enough to know that some Soldier out there may, with maybe some encouragement from his buddies or with a little too much to drink, be guilty of "alligator harassment."

We all, believe it or not, live in "alligator infested waters." We live in a world filled with many situations, substances and even some people who need to be avoided. Far too many of us constantly get into trouble and get hurt doing things we have no business doing, hanging out in places where we have no business being and being involved with some friends or being in relationships which, sooner or later, are going to come back to "bite" us.

The best way to deal with alligators is simply to back off and leave them alone. Just stay clear. When we realize that we are in dangerous "waters," we must not continue to hang out, feed the danger, or even play around at a risk to our lives, our families, our careers, or our wellbeing. The problem with harassing alligators is that we will eventually get hurt and hurt all the ones who love us and who are loved by us. So, if you are messing around with deadly substances, risking all in dangerous situations, or involved in any harmful relationships, stop! Pay attention to the warning signs and get out of there. If not, you and everyone you care about are guaranteed to get hurt. The lasting pain is never worth the temporary pleasure and short lived fun of harassing your alligators.

R&R
Rewind & Review

REVIEW QUESTIONS:

1. Contrast our real purpose in life to the empty purposes that Satan tricks people to live for so that they waste their lives and eternities:

2. In Joshua 1:9, what are some keys that helped Joshua and can help us when we feel overwhelmed?

3. What are some of Satan's lies that he tells you and how can you respond to those lies to help guard your mind and thoughts?

MRE: "Are you Committed or Involved?"

May I ask you a question? Are you committed or just involved? Commitment means giving 110% of ourselves to someone or to something else. A total commitment is an essential element in enjoying a successful marriage, family life, career, and especially in enjoying a right relationship with Jesus Christ. Far too many people want to be involved in a relationship but not be committed. The difference between being committed or involved can be found in the different level of sacrifice a pig and a chicken make in providing a ham and eggs breakfast. The pig would be totally committed while the chicken would only be slightly involved.

Many people want to enjoy the blessings of God and of family without being committed to either. I have counseled with a number of soldiers who wanted to be married, enjoy their children, and receive BAH or live in housing, but who also wanted to live their own lives, without their spouse and with someone else. Imagine my response and the chances of survival for their marriages. A lasting and healthy marriage requires a total commitment. Neither this old chaplain nor my wife (the "hot blonde babe") would be satisfied with anything less than a total 110% commitment from the other.

Just as a healthy marriage requires a total commitment on our part, so does a healthy relationship with God. Jesus made the ultimate sacrifice and commitment to us on the cross and He is deserving of the same kind of love and commitment from us. We can't live for God and live for ourselves (do our own thing without God) at the same time. Many people want to be involved with God (be forgiven, go to heaven, enjoy His love and blessings, even go to chapel/church if they can't find anything else better to do) without being committed to Christ (loving Him, serving Him, obeying His Word, living for Him 24/7). Jesus deserves our very best and is not satisfied with anything less.

So today, don't just be involved spiritually and end up giving God a goose egg, give Him your whole heart, all your love and commit your life to Him every day! If you do, then you will truly be able to enjoy the riches of His love and His blessings upon you, your family and upon your future. Remember that success in the eyes of God is not based upon dollar signs, but upon our level of commitment to Him. Don't try to just be involved, be committed!

Full Battle Rattle

(R-Resist)

When you go to war you don't go in your shorts and flip flops or in civilian clothes, you go in "full battle rattle." Full battle rattle includes: Uniform, boots, helmet, web gear, flack vest with plates, and locked and loaded weapons (Bibles for us chaplains). "Full battle rattle" can be a little heavy and uncomfortable at times, but every piece is essential for our protection. Numerous lives were saved as enemy bullets and pieces of shrapnel were harmlessly deflected. Most soldiers were thankful to have that extra protection.

The Apostle Paul describes our spiritual protective armor in Ephesians 6:13-18. He may have been chained to a Roman soldier and used his armor as an illustration of the Armor of God. Paul writes:

Therefore put on the full armor of God, so that when the day of evil comes, you may be able to stand your ground, and after you have done everything, to stand. Stand firm then, with the belt of truth buckled around your waist, with the breastplate of righteousness in place, and with your feet fitted with the readiness that comes from the gospel of peace. In addition to all this, take up the shield of faith, with which you can extinguish all the flaming arrows of the evil one. Take the helmet of salvation and the sword of the Spirit, which is the word of God. And pray in the Spirit on all occasions with all kinds of prayers and requests. With this in mind, be alert and always keep on praying for all the saints.

Our Spiritual uniform is:

Belt of Truth   (Web Gear)

Breastplate of Righteousness   (Flack vest)

Feet shod with protection of the Gospel of Peace   (boots)

Shield of Faith	(armor)
Helmet of Salvation	(helmet)
Sword of the Spirit	(weapon)
Praying Always	(Commo)

Our spiritual full battle rattle is guaranteed to completely protect us from any satanic attack so it is essential for us to be sure to get fully dressed every morning. The belt of truth means knowing the truth of God's Word that protects against Satan's propaganda (lies and tricks). The "boots" of the Gospel of Peace means always being ready to share the good news of Christ's love and freedom with others. The shield of faith is trusting in God when Satan's RPGs of doubt and temptation come our way. The helmet of salvation means knowing we belong to Christ, which guards our minds against Satan's intrusive thoughts of doubt. The sword of the Spirit is the Word of God and is our weapon to fight back against Satan's attacks. Every time Jesus was tempted, He responded with Scripture, "It is written." When Satan attacks, we can fight back with an appropriate Scripture. Finally we can always call for help and "air support" by praying and calling on God to help us stand strong. God answers prayer and will always come to our aid when we call for His help. Satan's insurgents will always run and hide whenever God comes to our rescue.

The best way to survive Satan's attacks is to always be in full battle rattle. Like any terrorist, Satan is always looking for a weakness or opening in our lives. Wearing the whole armor of God will not only protect us totally, it always leads to the enemy's total defeat.

BATTLE DRILLS: Practice by faith putting on the whole armor of God:

1. Truth:
    John 8:32: Then you will know the truth, and the truth will set you free."

    Psalm 119:11: Your Word have I hid in my heart that I might not sin against you.

2. Righteousness:
    Matthew: 6:33: But seek first his kingdom and his righteousness, and all these things will be given to you as well.

3. Gospel:
    Mark 16:15: He said to them, "Go into all the world and preach the good news to all creation.

4. Faith:
    Proverbs: 3:5-6: Trust in the Lord with all your heart and lean not on your own understanding; in all your ways acknowledge him, and he will make your paths straight.

5. Salvation:
    John 20:31: But these are written that you may believe that Jesus is the Christ, the Son of God, and that by believing you may have life in his name.

6. Word of God:
    Hebrews 4:12: For the word of God is living and active. Sharper than any double-edged sword …

7. Prayer:
    1 Thessalonians 5:16-18: Be joyful always; pray continually; give thanks in all circumstances, for this is God's will for you in Christ Jesus.

COMMO CHECK:

Talk to God and ask Him to help you be ready for satanic attack. Ask Him to help you know the truth, to stay right with Him, to share the good news of His love with others, to trust in Him totally, thank Him for saving you, and to help you know His Word and to always be in constant communication with Him through prayer.

MRE: "Got a Nickel?"

One day I was in the checkout line at Lowes, after finishing my manly-man shopping duties. I picked a nickel out of a handful of change to give to the cashier, but immediately I could tell something was just not right. This nickel was gray and plastic. This nickel was no nickel at all. This nickel was a worthless fake and a cheap imitation. Immediately, I grabbed a real nickel and gave it to the cashier. As I left, I wondered who could have given me a fake nickel and how could I have been so easily fooled?

In life, we always have to be on the lookout for fakes, counterfeits and cheap imitations. This is especially true spiritually. Satan is a master counterfeiter. He will always try to trick us into falling for cheap imitations and fakes instead of receiving the real riches of God. He will tempt us to choose lust instead of love, works instead of God's grace, cults instead of Christ, worldly riches instead of heavenly rewards, and the temporary pleasures of sin instead of the eternal blessings of righteousness. Be careful what you choose. Make sure to choose that which will be of lasting and eternal value instead of things, which, in the end, will leave you feeling worthless and empty. If you don't know what choice to make, you can always search God's Word, pray and ask WWJD? WWJD is far more than just a bumper sticker, bracelet, necklace or a keychain ornament; WWJD is the only way to live a meaningful life!

Shock and Awe

(R-Resist)

A major part of the strategy for the liberation of Iraq included "shock and awe." "Shock and awe" was not a father's response to his daughter's new tattoo or boyfriend, but a plan to saturate the enemy with our airpower to help break their will to fight when we crossed the border. The plan called for the launching of some 800 cruise missile air strikes by our Air Force and Navy in conjunction with a ground assault by our Soldiers and Marines. The goal was to totally overwhelm the Iraqi army so that they would either quickly surrender or lay down their weapons and melt away. An all-out offensive also provided the best self-defense: you can attack and move forward, or you wait to be attacked. Casualties are usually much higher when we are on the defense, waiting for the enemy to hit us, than when we are taking the fight to the enemy.

The best spiritual battle plan against satanic temptation and attack is a "shock and awe" battle plan. Far too many Christians are living life on the defense. Often, because we have tasted defeat in the past, we dig in and are afraid to move on and try again. A far better plan is to go on the attack by saturating and filling our lives, hearts and minds (the spiritual battlefield) with Christ. Here are a few suggestions of our spiritual Shock and Awe battle plan:

1. Start every day with Christ: Through morning devotions, prayer and scripture reading

2. Reading the Bible and good Christian books.

3. Listening to Christian music.

4. Continually focus your thoughts on Christ by meditating on Him

5. Spending time with good Christian friends

6. Staying busy serving others

OPERATION ETERNAL FREEDOM

7. Faithfully attending and worshipping in a chapel or church

8. Continual surrender to God's Holy Spirit as your Commander

9. Continual separation/staying away from temptations or sin

10. Continual thanking God for His goodness and grace in your life

The goal of our battle plan is to fill our hearts and lives with Christ so that we will have no desire or room for anything the devil has to offer. Also Satan is terrified in the presence of God and will not fight when he knows he's "out-gunned." An all-out 100% commitment to Christ every day and saturating every area of life with God and godly things is the best defense against satanic attacks.

BATTLE DRILLS:

Psalm 42:1-2: As the deer pants for streams of water, so my soul pants for you, O God. My soul thirsts for God, for the living God. When can I go and meet with God?

Psalm 63:1-2: O God, you are my God, earnestly I seek you; my soul thirsts for you, my body longs for you, in a dry and weary land where there is no water. I have seen you in the sanctuary and beheld your power and your glory.

Mathew 5:6: Blessed are those who hunger and thirst for righteousness, for they will be filled.

Ephesians 5:17-20: Therefore do not be foolish, but understand what the Lord's will is. Do not get drunk on wine, which leads to debauchery. Instead, be filled with the Spirit. Speak to one another with psalms, hymns and spiritual songs. Sing and make music in your heart to the Lord, always giving thanks to God the Father for everything, in the name of our Lord Jesus Christ.

1. What does it mean to "hunger," "thirst," and be "filled" with God?

2. What difference does God make in my life and heart when I fill my life with Him?

COMMO CHECK:

Talk to God and ask Him to help you totally saturate your life with Jesus and to always want to know more about Jesus and draw closer to Him.

MRE: "God at Work"

Awhile back, my wife went to visit her sister in the mountains of Southwest Virginia. She brought back this old end table she had found in an abandoned, run-down shack on the side of a mountain. This table was probably homemade about 40 years ago and was covered by years of dirt and several coats of paint. It was falling apart and looked totally worthless. Being a manly, man, I decided to fix this table so I went to Wal-Mart and bought a high-powered sander. As I went to work, dust and paint chips filled the air in my garage.

Two hours and three sanding pads later, the table was finally clean and ready to be refinished. Why did I work so hard on a dirty, worthless table? This table belonged to my wife's father. So, even though it was worthless to others, the table was extremely valuable to her. A beautiful table now stands in my dining room as a wonderful testimony to my work.

As I was sanding the table, I was reminded of how God often works on us. God is the Expert in taking, broken-down and even dirty lives which may appear worthless to others and making them brand new. The work of God, as He sands off our rough edges or grinds down our pride, may seem to unpleasant or even painful at times, but God will continue His work until we are one day perfected in His presence. Why does God go through so much trouble? God loves us, we are truly valuable to Him and we belong to His Son. One day, in heaven, we will be an eternal testimony to the work of God in us!

"For we are God's workmanship created in Christ Jesus ..." (Ephesians 2:10).

Overcoming Adversity
(R-Resist)

After three months of waiting in the desert of Northern Kuwait, we were as ready to go to war as we could possibly be. We were packed, prepped, loaded, and ready to go. For once the chaplain had the best vehicle in the battalion. I even had my own radio. "Buffalo Shepherd's" Humvee was quite the ride. The back seats were laid down to make way for my bed, made with a sheet of plywood and foam padding. We had a month's supply of MREs, water, thirty extra gallons of fuel and enough snacks and goodies to last for weeks to come. We were definitely ready to go.

Buffalo Shepherd's ride did great for the first 20 hours of the war when, through no fault of our own, our Humvee became our battalion's first combat loss. The attack on the Iraqi Air Base at Tallil had just begun when my Humvee was crushed by a tracked vehicle which raced from behind us in the dark. The track ended up sitting on top of our now completely smashed vehicle with me, my chaplain's assistant and a Wall Street Journal reporter inside. Even though our Humvee was completely destroyed, miraculously, I crawled out unharmed. I was then able to pull my Chaplain's Assistant and the Wall Street Journal reporter out and then continue on the mission riding in the back of another vehicle. Strangely, for some reason, the reporter decided that she had seen enough of combat and soon returned back home.

We had started off great, but in the heat of battle, lost our vehicle, our food, our water and most of our gear and personal belongings which had been destroyed or left behind as we moved on with the assault. We had been shaken up and a little bruised, but were thankful to be alive. What could we do now? We couldn't go home, we couldn't go back, and we couldn't quit. We didn't have a choice seeing how the battle was raging on and we were in the middle of Iraq. We grabbed what little we could carry, jumped into the back of another vehicle and rode the rest of the way to Baghdad with our battalion medics. War is like that. It seldom goes as we planned. Combat losses happen, but the fight must go on. Even when you find yourself crushed, bruised and bleeding, you have to get up and keep on fighting.

Spiritual combat is like that, too. What do you do when, in spite of your commitment, promises, preparation, prayers and plans, you find yourself crushed by failure? Your fight might have been going fine, but you were blindsided by temptation or were a victim of "friendly fire." What can you do? You can't go back. You can't quit and you can't surrender to Satan as the war still rages on. Even though you may be bruised, in shock, angry with yourself, embarrassed or ashamed, you can't give up. Let Jesus help you up, care for your wounds and get back into the fight. His grace is sufficient and his love will carry you through until the war is over.

Resisting the devil means you don't ever stop fighting back. You have to keep on fighting even when everything falls apart and, from time to time, you taste the bitterness of failure. Failure doesn't have to be final. You have to keep on trying, no matter how many times or how hard you fall. If you want to move forward, you have to let go of your past. Get back up, trust in Christ, and remember, "The battle is the Lord's."

BATTLE DRILLS:

Psalm 51:1-13: Have mercy on me, O God, according to your unfailing love; according to your great compassion blot out my transgressions. Wash away all my iniquity and cleanse me from my sin. For I know my transgressions, and my sin is always before me. Against you, you only, have I sinned and done what is evil in your sight, so that you are proved right when you speak and justified when you judge. Surely I was sinful at birth, sinful from the time my mother conceived me. Surely you desire truth in the inner parts; you teach me wisdom in the inmost place. Cleanse me with hyssop, and I will be clean; wash me, and I will be whiter than snow. Let me hear joy and gladness; let the bones you have crushed rejoice. Hide your face from my sins and blot out all my iniquity. Create in me a pure heart, O God, and renew a steadfast spirit within me. Do not cast me from your presence or take your Holy Spirit from me. Restore to me the joy of your salvation and grant me a willing spirit, to sustain me. Then I will teach transgressors your ways, and sinners will turn back to you.

1 John 1:8-2:2: If we claim to be without sin, we deceive ourselves and the truth is not in us. If we confess our sins, he is faithful and just and will forgive us our sins and purify us from all unrighteousness. If we claim we have not sinned, we make him out to be a liar and his word has no place in our lives. My dear children, I write this to you so that you will not sin. But if anybody does sin, we have one who speaks to the Father in our defense--Jesus Christ, the Righteous One. He is the atoning sacrifice for our sins, and not only for ours but also for the sins of the whole world.

1. How do we receive forgiveness from God?

2. What should we do once God forgives us?

COMMO CHECK:

Talk to God and ask Him to forgive you whenever you fall into sin and to help you back up again. Thank Him for ALWAYS forgiving you and for ALWAYS loving you.

MRE: "Perfect!"

As a hospital chaplain I was often asked a number of questions as I made my rounds. These questions were usually about God, faith, religious practices, family relationships or about a patient's care. The question asked most often was, "Chaplain, how is that grand-baby doing?" To which I always smiled and responded, "Perfect!" I would then go on to show the latest videos and pictures of "Big Nate" and now all four of my grandsons on my cell phone. While Nathaniel (Big Nate) was a normal baby boy with dirty diapers and an occasional attitude, in my eyes, he was always perfect. To me, Nathaniel was the best, smartest and most beautiful baby in the entire world and if you don't believe me, I will show you the pictures and videos to prove it! In my eyes, Nathaniel, Tony, Blake and Jacob will always be perfect because they will always be my grandsons. I will always love them and nothing will ever change that.

Today I have some good news for you. In the eyes of your Heavenly Father, you are perfect! Through faith in Christ and His atoning death on the cross for our sins, we have been adopted as a child of God. God has chosen to make you His very own precious child, He is perfecting you and He is committed to love you forever and nothing will ever change how He feels about you. God always loves us in spite of our "dirty diapers" and little attitudes. To Him, you are the best, the smartest and the most beautiful child in the entire world. Your Heavenly Father doesn't need a camera phone. He is watching over you in love constantly. So even though at times you may feel like you fail Him miserably, just remember that in God's eyes, you are perfect!

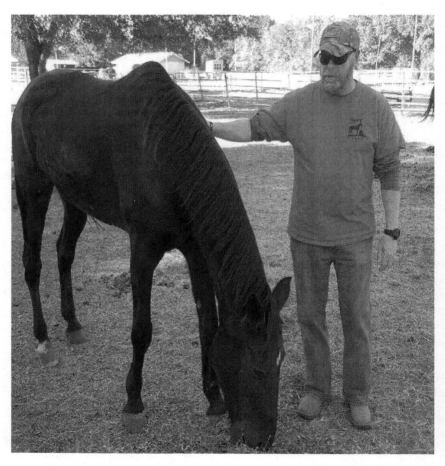

TROGDON WITH ONE OF HIS HORSES ON HIS THERAPY RANCH

No Weekend Warriors

(E-Experiencing God)

Ever since 9-11 life in the military has changed. There was a time when soldiers in the Army Reserves or National Guard were regarded as "Weekend Warriors" with little chance of ever seeing combat alongside of us "real soldiers." Now, Reservists and Guardsmen play a vital role in the War on Terror. Our engineer battalion was joined by a Reserve bridge company from West Virginia which crossed the border right along with us. One young soldier literally went from being a manager at Wal-Mart to combat almost overnight. In today's Army there is no such thing as a "weekend warrior." In Iraq or Afghanistan, you have to be a soldier 24/7 because your life and the lives of your buddies depend on it. In combat, you can't take a day or a weekend off and you definitely can't be only a "weekend warrior."

Far too many Christians try to serve God as "weekend warriors." Christianity is not just going to church on Sunday or every Christmas or Easter (whether you think you need it or not), Christianity is a personal relationship with Christ. The Christian life is a 24/7 relationship with God. One hour on Sunday morning sitting in chapel or church will not result in spiritual victory over temptation, lasting freedom, or the abundant and joyful life that God wants us to experience every day. Just as we need to eat, drink and truly enjoy a good meal every day, Jesus said, "Blessed are those who hunger and thirst for righteousness for they will be filled" (Matthew 5:6).

People try to fill their empty lives and hearts with drugs, alcohol, porn, gambling, material things, money, success, work, unhealthy relationships, and numerous other things and destructive behaviors which only will lead to pain, slavery and bondage. Why? People hope to feel better, escape from pain, deal with difficult times and fill the emptiness in their hearts that only a right relationship with Jesus can truly fill. It is not enough to just try to stop doing a destructive behavior; we must start filling our lives with Christ. The only way to truly end a negative addiction is to fill the void left behind with a positive "addiction" -- the love and life of Christ.

Just as a young couple in love can't seem to get enough of each other, spending hours on the phone and cherishing every moment together, a relationship with God will result in a life filled with love for Christ. A life filled with Christ every day will result in joy, hope and help as well as lasting satisfaction and true meaning. A person who fills their life with Christ will have no need or desire to fill their empty heart or ease the pain with anything or anyone else. A heart filled with the love and presence of God will have no need for satanic substitutes in order to try to feel better or to cope with the problems of life.

How do we fill our lives with Christ? The path to freedom is a daily walk with Christ!

We must separate ourselves from sin and start saturating our lives with Christ by starting every day with prayer (talking to God), reading the Bible (listening to God), personal worship (expressing love and thanks to God), and trying our best to live every moment of every day in a way that pleases God. Daily spiritual saturation can also include listening to good Christian music, reading good Christian books and looking for ways to serve others. Once we start filling our lives with the love of God, we will begin to start enjoying the freedom He has provided in a daily relationship with Jesus. A little bit of God in your life won't set you free, but giving God your all definitely will. So, no more weekend warriors! Commit your life totally to Christ and join the fight for freedom daily!

BATTLE DRILLS:

Psalm 9:1: I will praise you, O Lord, with all my heart; I will tell of all your wonders.

Matthew 5:6: Blessed are those who hunger and thirst for righteousness, for they will be filled.

Matthew 22:37: Jesus replied: "Love the Lord your God with all your heart and with all your soul and with all your mind."

Luke 9:23: Then he said to them all: "If anyone would come after me, he must deny himself and take up his cross daily and follow me.

Acts 2:46-47: Every day they continued to meet together in the temple courts. They broke bread in their homes and ate together with glad and sincere hearts, praising God and enjoying the favor of all the people. And the Lord added to their number daily those who were being saved.

Acts 17:11: Now the Bereans were of more noble character than the Thessalonians, for they received the message with great eagerness and examined the Scriptures every day to see if what Paul said was true.

Ephesians 5:17-20: Therefore do not be foolish, but understand what the Lord's will is. Do not get drunk on wine, which leads to debauchery. Instead, be filled with the Spirit. Speak to one another with psalms, hymns and spiritual songs. Sing and make music in your heart to the Lord, always giving thanks to God the Father for everything, in the name of our Lord Jesus Christ.

Romans 1:9: God, whom I serve with my whole heart in preaching the gospel of his Son, is my witness how constantly I remember you.

2 Timothy 1:3: I thank God, whom I serve, as my forefathers did, with a clear conscience, as night and day I constantly remember you in my prayers.

Hebrews 3:13: But encourage one another daily, as long as it is called today, so that none of you may be hardened by sin's deceitfulness.

1. **What are some things we should do every day in our service to God?**

2. **What are some things we should do with all our heart?**

COMMO CHECK:

Talk to God and give Him your life today. Ask Him to help you live for and love Him every day.

MRE: "Paid in Full"

I heard about a man in Malaysia who received a bill from the phone company for $218,000,000. The phone company informed him that if he didn't pay up immediately that he would be taken to court. Now we know that this bill had to be a mistake as no one could run up a phone bill to $218,000,000, although, if it wasn't for having unlimited minutes, my wife could come close on her cell phone. So, hopefully the telephone company and this poor indebted man will be able to resolve his phone bill.

Many people don't realize it, but due to our own sin and spiritual failures; we owed God a debt far greater than $218,000,000. We owed a spiritual debt to God that we could never repay, not even in 218,000,000 years. Because of our guilt and overwhelming debt of sin, we were sentenced by a holy Judge to eternal separation from God in hell. What could we do? Nothing on our own, but that is why Good Friday is so good for us. On that first Good Friday, our Lord and Savior Jesus Christ went to the cross, took our place, and paid our sin debt in full. Through faith in Christ, we receive complete forgiveness, full payment for all our sin and eternal life. His pain was truly your gain!

"Jesus paid it all, All to Him I owe; Sin had left a crimson stain, He washed it white as snow!" (Elvina Hall)

"Baghdad Bob"

(E-Experiencing God)

Do you remember Bob? Back in 2003, many of us were introduced to Bob on Fox News, CNN or one of the other major news networks at the beginning of the war. While Bob wasn't his real name, he will ever be known as "Baghdad Bob" the Minister of Iraqi Information (disinformation). I first "met" Baghdad Bob shortly after the 3rd Infantry Division took over the airport. We changed the name from "Saddam International" to "Bush International" until it was renamed as Baghdad International Airport. We first saw Bob on an Iraqi television, which one of our mechanics had found and rigged to work off the power in his tracked vehicle. We laughed as we turned on the TV to find Bob standing there briefing the American press. Imagine our surprise when we heard Bob say, "There are no American soldiers at the airport. The infidels invaded and we slit their throats. We are in complete control of the airport." There we were at the airport watching someone tell the world that we had failed, had been defeated and had even been killed in our attempts to try to take the airport. While we laughed, I remembered wondering how many people might actually believe the propaganda of a clearly desperate and defeated enemy.

While we saw Bob as being fairly harmless and even a joke, Satan is a far more dangerous "minister of disinformation." Even though Satan is a defeated enemy, he is constantly lying, deceiving, controlling and destroying millions of people with his false propaganda. His lies include:

1. There is no God. Life is all about you, so enjoy it while you can.

2. It doesn't matter who or what you believe in as long as you are sincere.

3. God will never forgive you. Look at how many times you have failed.

4. It is not your fault. God made you this way.

5. God will only forgive you if you promise to never do it again and prove it.

6. God understands and always forgives, so go ahead and do it.

7. You will never change so, why keep trying?

The best defense against deception is to know the truth. What is truth? Jesus is truth! He said, "Then you will know the truth, and the truth will set you free" (John 8:32).

Jesus is the only way to live and the only way to heaven. Jesus is the ultimate Truth and the ultimate life. True freedom can only be found in Him alone. To know Him is to know and experience truth, life and freedom. His truth always defeats the false propaganda of the devil.

1. "And without faith it is impossible to please God, because anyone who comes to him must believe that he exists and that he rewards those who earnestly seek him" (Hebrews 11:6).

2. "I am the way, and the truth and the life. No one comes to the Father except through me" (John 14:6).

3. "If we confess our sins, he is faithful and just and will forgive us our sins and purify us from all unrighteousness" (1 John 1:9).

4. "When tempted, no one should say, 'God is tempting me'…but each one is tempted when by his own evil desire, he is dragged away and enticed" (James 1:13-14).

5. "For it has by grace you have been saved, through faith—and this not from yourselves, it is the gift of God—not by works, so that no one can boast" (Ephesians 2:8-9).

6. "What shall we say then? Shall we go on sinning so that grace may increase? By no means! We died to sin; how can we live in it any longer?" (Romans 6: 1-2)

7. "Therefore, if anyone is in Christ, he is a new creation; the old has gone, the new has come!" (2 Corinthians 5:17). "I can do everything through him who gives me strength" (Philippians 4:13).

The good news of the Gospel is that God loves you with an everlasting love and nothing can ever change that. Jesus died for your sins so that you could be forgiven and He has promised to forgive you no matter how many times you may fail. Jesus has promised to set you free and help you enjoy that freedom and to help you live in victory. Satan has already lost so don't listen to his attempts to discourage, demoralize and defeat you with his lies. "So if the Son sets you free, you will be free indeed" (John 8:36).

BATTLE DRILLS:

Genesis 3:1-5: Now the serpent was more crafty than any of the wild animals the Lord God had made. He said to the woman, "Did God really say, 'You must not eat from any tree in the garden'?" The woman said to the serpent, "We may eat fruit from the trees in the garden, but God did say, 'You must not eat fruit from the tree that is in the middle of the garden, and you must not touch it, or you will die.'" "You will not surely die," the serpent said to the woman. "For God knows that when you eat of it your eyes will be opened, and you will be like God, knowing good and evil."

Psalm 119:160: All your words are true; all your righteous laws are eternal.

John 8:44: You belong to your father, the devil, and you want to carry out your father's desire. He was a murderer from the beginning, not holding to the truth, for there is no truth in him. When he lies, he speaks his native language, for he is a liar and the father of lies

Revelation 20:10: And the devil, who deceived them, was thrown into the lake of burning sulfur, where the beast and the false prophet had been thrown. They will be tormented day and night forever and ever.

1. **What do these Scriptures tell us about the devil and his propaganda?**

2.   What do these Scriptures tell us about the devil's future?

3.   How important is it to know the truth?

COMMO CHECK:

Talk to God and ask Him to help you to reject the Devil's lies and propaganda and to know His truth that always sets you free.

MRE: "Freedom is Not Free"

One of my favorite places to visit in Washington DC is the Korean War Memorial. This lesser known memorial sets off to the side of the Mall near the Lincoln Memorial. The Korean War Memorial honors all those who fought and died in the Korean War and features 19 statues. These statues are approximately 7'3" tall and represent 14 Soldiers, 3 Marines, 1 Sailor and 1 Airman walking in formation across the rugged Korean countryside. At the front of the memorial engraved on a wall one can find these words, "Freedom is not Free." For those of us served in Combat, we far too often witnessed the high price of freedom up close and personal. Freedom always comes at a cost. Our political, personal, religious and spiritual freedoms have all been purchased with the blood of others. As Christians and Believers, our eternal freedom was bought with the very blood of Jesus Christ and His sacrifice for our sins on the Cross. Let's be sure to always thank God for our Savior and to always remember that Freedom is not free!

"Then you shall know the truth and the truth shall set you free" (John 8:32).

"This is Buffalo Shepherd, over"

(E-Experiencing God)

Sometimes, with a little help or due to our own stupidity, we get ourselves into a whole lot of trouble. This happened to me just a couple days into the war outside of Nasiriyah. This was the day two medics, a chaplain's assistant and an unarmed chaplain drove all over the battlefield looking for an ambulance exchange point which we later found out, didn't exist. After finally dropping off an injured soldier at Charlie Med, we began the long trip back to our site. I called in to our battalion to let them know that "Buffalo Shepherd" was on the way back. We were immediately informed that our team had to move out due to a large number of Fedayeen who were operating in the same area where we had been the night before. I asked for the grid to our new location and we headed out.

Upon arriving at our "new" location, we soon discovered that we had been sent right back to where we had been before. We found ourselves alone and in the dark somewhere where we had no business being. We called in for another grid and were told to wait there until someone could come and get us. A few minutes later, my assistant, who was watching through his night vision goggles, noticed six Fedayeen about 100 meters to our south. They seemed to be watching and wondering about what we were doing. A little while later, we heard and saw an enemy tracked-vehicle about 100 meters to our North. The track had its headlights on and was slowly making its way in our direction. We radioed back in and were told that help was on the way and to stay put. We couldn't fire because we knew we were outgunned and outnumbered.

While there was much we couldn't do, there was something we could do. Ultimately, it was the best and most powerful weapon in our arsenal. I prayed. I prayed for God's protection and I prayed for God to help us. I kept praying and just in time, God answered. The track that had been slowly moving toward us suddenly stopped, turned off its lights and headed off. The Fedayeen to our South had also disappeared.

That was when we saw a convoy of American vehicles approaching. We immediately moved out and were able to join back up with our unit at about 0200 in the morning. We were thankful to be safe and alive.

While good communications are essential on the battlefield, continual communication with God is even more vital. Prayer is not just repeating "holy" words or phrases with our heads bowed or down on our knees, prayer is our personal communication with God Himself. Prayer is talking with God. Prayer is our means of entering into the presence and accessing the power of the omnipotent (all-powerful) God of the universe. When we pray, we enter into the very spiritual presence of God. He hears our every word and always answers. While God may not give us everything we ask for exactly when we want it, He will always give us everything we need exactly when we need it. Also, while it is possible to lose commo on the battlefield or to get out of range, we can never get to a place in our lives where God can't hear our cries for help. Be sure to follow the "orders" of the Apostle Paul and "don't stop praying."

BATTLE DRILLS:

Matthew 6:9-13: "This, then, is how you should pray: "'Our Father in heaven, hallowed be your name, your kingdom come, your will be done on earth as it is in heaven. Give us today our daily bread. Forgive us our debts, as we also have forgiven our debtors. And lead us not into temptation, but deliver us from the evil one.

Matthew 26:41: "Watch and pray so that you will not fall into temptation. The spirit is willing, but the body is weak."

Romans 8:26: In the same way, the Spirit helps us in our weakness. We do not know what we ought to pray for, but the Spirit himself intercedes for us with groans that words cannot express

Ephesians 6:18-19: And pray in the Spirit on all occasions with all kinds of prayers and requests. With this in mind, be alert and always keep on praying for all the saints. Pray also for me, that whenever I open my mouth, words may be given me so that I will fearlessly make known the mystery of the gospel.

1 Thessalonians 5:17: Pray continually;

James 5:13-18: Is any one of you in trouble? He should pray. Is anyone happy? Let him sing songs of praise. Is any one of you sick? He should call the elders of the church to pray over him and anoint him with oil in the name of the Lord. And the prayer offered in faith will make the sick person well; the Lord will raise him up. If he has sinned, he will be forgiven. Therefore confess your sins to each other and pray for each other so that you may be healed. The prayer of a righteous man is powerful and effective. Elijah was a man just like us. He prayed earnestly that it would not rain, and it did not rain on the land for three and a half years. Again he prayed, and the heavens gave rain, and the earth produced its crops.

1. **According to these Scriptures, what are some things we should pray about?**

2. **How often should we pray?**

3. **What can we expect to happen when we pray?**

COMMO CHECK:

Talk to God and ask Him to help you to remember to pray at all times about everything. Thank Him for always answering your prayers, even when He says, "No" or "Not yet."

MRE: "Who are You Talking To?"

Recently I noticed a young lady who was clearly with child walking across a parking lot. I noticed that she was talking to someone, but she was alone. I immediately began to wonder who she was talking to and I came up with a number of possibilities:

1. Most likely, she had a cell phone earpiece in her other ear which I couldn't see and that would be okay.

2. She could have been talking to her unborn baby which would also have been okay.

3. She could have been talking to herself which would kind of been okay (since I do this sometimes too).

4. She could have been talking to someone who wasn't there and that wouldn't have been so okay.

5. She could have been talking to God which would have been more than okay.

Many times, people have the wrong idea when it comes to prayer. Many people think prayer only involves repeating those "holy" phrases when we are down on our knees with our eyes closed shut and our hands folded in front of us. Ultimately, prayer is simply talking to God. Prayer is going to your Heavenly Father with anything you want or need to talk to Him about. Prayer is spending time with the God of the universe who loves you dearly and who just wants to be with you. Prayer is asking for God's help and thanking Him for all the help He gives you every day. Prayer is focusing on God instead of on ourselves. Prayer should be as natural for the Christian as breathing, and is just as necessary.

So, today and every day, make sure that you take time out to pray and talk to the One who loves you far more than anyone else could ever love you and who hears you whenever you call on Him. By the way, if you are driving, be sure NOT to close your eyes when you pray. It is okay to talk to him as you drive down the highway or even when you walk across the parking lot.

R&R

Rewind and Review

Review Questions:

1. What is the only "offensive weapon" in the Armor of God and how can we be better qualified to use it?

2. What lies has Satan used against you and what Scripture/Spiritual truths can you use to defeat those lies?

3. What is prayer and what is the "right way" to pray? Is there a r
    way to pray?

MRE: "A Burp and a Blessing"

I love and have always loved babies. Soon after my first grandson arrived, I began to work out my "Papa Theology." One night, as I was feeding Nathaniel, I was reminded of how helpless infants and little children really are. They are totally dependent upon their parents (and grandparents) for everything: for food, clothes, shelter, for protection, for love, and on and on and on. Babies are totally helpless without someone to love them and to care for them. You know I finished feeding Big Nate and he didn't even say, "Thank you," unless you count the burp. That's okay, I loved him anyway.

Whether we realize it or not, we are totally dependent upon our Heavenly Father for food, health, strength, protection, life, eternal life, and on and on and on. Everything we are and everything we have comes from God. Jesus said, "I tell you the truth, unless you change and become like little children, you will never enter the kingdom of heaven" (Matthew 18:3). When we realize just how much we really need Jesus for everything and put our faith in Him as our Lord and Savior, only then will we find and truly enjoy life, eternal life and the love of our Heavenly Father. So, today as you enjoy all the blessings of God, be sure to thank your Heavenly Father with more than just a burp. But if you forget, He will love you anyway.

Light in the Dark

(E-Encouraging Others)

One of the advantages of being a part of a high tech Army is that we "own the night." Our whole time in Iraq I found our NVGs (night vision goggles) to be a great blessing. I remember watching in awe as we crossed the 7-kilometer border between Kuwait and Iraq, as we began our mission to liberate Iraq, being able to see the minefields and obstacles all around even in the dark of night. The night was no obstacle and even provided us with a real advantage over an enemy who we could see but who couldn't see us. NVGs enabled us to move, to fight and to survive on a dangerous and dark battlefield. What a blessing and a lifesaver!

Spiritually, we live in a dark and dangerous world. Satan has set out his satanic "IEDs," demonic snipers and ambushes of temptation waiting to attack us and to cause us to become spiritual casualties in his war against God and against our freedom in Christ. The good news is that God has provided us with His spiritual "NVGs" to help us survive and thrive on the battlefield of life. Satan has been using the same old strategies for thousands of years. He uses the same tactics against us that he used against Adam and Eve in the garden almost 6,000 years ago. He distorted God's Word; he lied to them, tempted them with pleasure, and appealed to their pride ("you shall be like God knowing good and evil"). Adam and Eve blindly fell into his trap and millions still do today. Why? Because they are not able to see how he works and the traps which he has set for them.

The Word of God, the Bible, acts as our spiritual NVGs helping us to clearly see the traps and tactics of the devil and how to walk and live as we move forward in our fight for freedom. David (as in David and Goliath) wrote, "Your Word is a lamp unto my feet and a light unto my path." Spending time with God and reading the Bible every day will help us to grow to know more about God, and will also help us to be able to see more clearly how to live for God and fight against the devil's tricks and schemes. Just as NVGs use the light of the stars and moon to give us light in the darkness, God's Holy Spirit uses the light of the Son to shine through the pages of God's Word to give us spiritual light in a dark and sinful world.

So, before you take another step, which might lead you into a satanic minefield, open God's Word and use His light to guide you safely all the way home.

BATTLE DRILLS:

Psalm 119:9-11: How can a young man keep his way pure? By living according to your word. I seek you with all my heart; do not let me stray from your commands. I have hidden your word in my heart that I might not sin against you.

Psalm 119:103-105: How sweet are your words to my taste, sweeter than honey to my mouth! I gain understanding from your precepts; therefore I hate every wrong path. Your word is a lamp to my feet and a light for my path.

Colossians 3:16: Let the word of Christ dwell in you richly as you teach and admonish one another with all wisdom, and as you sing psalms, hymns and spiritual songs with gratitude in your hearts to God.

2 Timothy 3:15-17: ...and how from infancy you have known the holy Scriptures, which are able to make you wise for salvation through faith in Christ Jesus. All Scripture is God-breathed and is useful for teaching, rebuking, correcting and training in righteousness, so that the man of God may be thoroughly equipped for every good work.

Hebrews 4:12: For the word of God is living and active. Sharper than any double-edged sword, it penetrates even to dividing soul and spirit, joints and marrow; it judges the thoughts and attitudes of the heart.

James 1:22: Do not merely listen to the word, and so deceive yourselves. Do what it says.

2 Peter 1:19: And we have the word of the prophets made more certain, and you will do well to pay attention to it, as to a light shining in a dark place, until the day dawns and the morning star rises in your hearts.

List the benefits of knowing and living by God's Word found in these Scriptures:

COMMO CHECK:

Talk to God and ask Him to help you read, understand and apply His Word in your life every day. Ask for Him to use His Word to change your life and to make you more like Jesus.

MRE: "Mirror, Mirror…"

The older I get, the more I try to avoid mirrors. The problem with my mirror is that it always tells me the truth. No matter how much time I spend on my hair, I still don't look like Brad Pitt. May I ask you a personal question? Do you like what you see when you look into the mirror? I am not asking if you think you are handsome or pretty, or about your hair or lack of hair, or how you compare to the Hollywood star, supermodel or professional athlete. I am asking how you feel about yourself. Do you like yourself? Do you have a positive self-image? Even more important, when God looks at you, what do you think He sees?

The key to a healthy self-image is not found in any self-help book, plastic surgery, and weight loss program or miracle pill. The real key to a having a proper self-image is found in knowing how God feels about you. When God looks at us, He sees someone whom He loves dearly. God knows our faults, our failures, our good points, our bad points and He still loves us with a passion. God's love is unconditional. He loves you just as much as He loves Billy Graham and even more than the life of His own Son (John 3:16). You are valuable and precious in His eyes. So, tomorrow morning when you look into the mirror, don't worry too much about how the world might see you without your makeup or uncombed hair, remember that as a child of God you are always beautiful to Him!

"Your love O Lord, reaches to the heavens …" (Psalm 36:5).

"Clean Your Weapon!"

(E-Encouraging Others)

Many people are surprised when they discover that chaplains go to war without a weapon. That's right; chaplains are not allowed to carry a weapon, even in combat. Even though it is not against my theology or personal beliefs to defend myself, chaplains are truly "noncombatants." How are chaplains to survive on a battlefield without a weapon? That is the role of the chaplain's assistant. Chaplain's assistants not only assist the chaplain in their duties, but also protect the chaplain on the battlefield. Chaplain's assistants are responsible for the safety and security of their chaplain at all times. That is why I was thankful to have a good old country boy from Montana, who always fired expert on the rifle range, to be my chaplain's assistant. A chaplain and assistant are to exist as a true Religious Support Team (RST). The chaplain's life is, in part, in the hands of their assistant.

Even though I had my faith in God, I still had to depend on my chaplain's assistant to help keep us both safe in Iraq. For this reason, every time we had a little time on our race to Baghdad, I would always tell my assistant, "Clean your weapon." As a prior-service NCO and an old soldier, I know the importance of keeping your weapon clean. The dirt and sand of Iraq made keeping a weapon clean and functional a real challenge but it was still a necessity. My assistant cleaned his weapon several times a day during our down times so that we knew it was ready to fire and possibly save our lives if needed.

We live in a dirty world. Sin and temptation abounds. Our lives can easily get contaminated and dirty just living from day to day. Sex is everywhere, on the Internet, television, videos, magazines, clubs, and in workplace conversations. Alcohol and drugs are also an easy find, at most restaurants, bars, clubs and even as we gather for social events. We don't even have to go to Vegas to gamble.

We are constantly bombarded by a worldly philosophy of "If it feels good, do it;" anything goes; do whatever it takes to get ahead; money equals happiness; and if your spouse is not meeting your wants, all you have to do is trade him or her in for a newer model. People don't realize that living for self is actually living for Satan. Following the world's advice will always leave us empty, hurting and dirty. It is almost impossible to watch television or spend much time online without being contaminated with ungodly attitudes and the philosophy and priorities of this world. A philosophy that "preaches" that I am the center of the universe and life is all about me.

We must do everything we can to stay clean and free from the dirt of this world. This is possible by staying away from all we know to be wrong and by continually receiving God's cleansing whenever we do fail. There are two Bible words which describe staying clean and living a clean and godly life, "holiness" and "righteousness." Holiness means being set apart and staying away from sin and from actions, attitudes or anything which would not be pleasing to a holy God. Sin makes us too dirty for God to use to help others or fight against the devil. Righteousness means to be right with God and to do all we can to live right and stay right with Him. Through our personal faith in Christ and His sacrificial death on the cross, we are made holy and righteous in the eyes of God. We, in response to His love and death for us, have the responsibility to do all we can to live holy and right for Him to the very best of our ability. God knows that we are far from perfect so He constantly forgives us and cleanses us as we confess our sins to Him. A life of continual separation from sin will help us to be happy, holy and a weapon which God can use in the spiritual war on terror!

BATTLE DRILLS:

Leviticus 11:45: I am the Lord who brought you up out of Egypt to be your God; therefore be holy, because I am holy.

Matthew 5:8: The pure in heart shall see God.

2 Corinthians 6:14-18: Do not be yoked together with unbelievers. For what do righteousness and wickedness have in common? Or what fellowship can light have with darkness? What harmony is there between Christ and Belial? What does a believer have in common with an unbeliever? What agreement is there between the temple of God and idols? For we are the temple of the living God. As God has said: "I will live with them and walk among them, and I will be their God, and they will be my people. Therefore come out from them and be separate, says the Lord. Touch no unclean thing, and I will receive you. I will be a Father to you, and you will be my sons and daughters, says the Lord Almighty."

2 Corinthians 7:1: Since we have these promises, dear friends, let us purify ourselves from everything that contaminates body and spirit, perfecting holiness out of reverence for God.

Hebrews 12:14: Make every effort to live in peace with all men and to be holy; without holiness no one will see the Lord.

1 Peter 1:16: for it is written: "Be holy, because I am holy."

List reasons why we should try to live holy lives?

COMMO CHECK:

Talk to God and ask Him to show you where you are not what you ought to be, to help you stay away from sin, and to help you be holy.

MRE: "AWOL Alligator"

A headline in a local newspaper read, "Alligator on the Run." The story told about a maintenance worker discovering a 4 ½ foot alligator in the basement of an apartment near our military post. While on the way to turn the alligator over to wildlife officers, somehow the alligator escaped off the back of the truck. Now, somewhere in the vicinity, we had an AWOL alligator on the loose.

Can you imagine having an alligator hiding in your basement or wandering around your neighborhood? Would that make a difference in how we lived? Would we call for help to get rid of the danger? Would we be more careful on our evening walk? Would we be on the lookout and more careful taking our children swimming or going fishing at a local pond? I am sure we would. Now that I live in Florida, I am always on the lookout for alligators, poisonous snakes, panthers, bobcats, bears and other dangerous "critters" in my Panhandle neighborhood.

While we should always be on guard against potential dangers around us, there is another far more dangerous "predator" which is always stalking his prey. The Apostle Peter writes, "Be sober, be vigilant; because your adversary the devil, as a roaring lion, walks about, seeking whom he may devour. Whom resist steadfast in the faith..." (1 Peter 5:8-9). Satan is far more dangerous than any alligator and Peter learned this the hard way. He devours lives, devastates families, damages futures and is never satisfied. Satan is not controlled by a rope, a net, duct tape or by some brave (crazy) hunter, but through our faith in Christ and our faithfulness to Him. So, keep your faith in Jesus who is the ultimate "lion tamer" and you will have nothing to worry about anything the devil sends your way.

Spiritual Combat Team

(E-Encouraging Others)

One of the greatest comforts of being in combat is found in knowing that you are not fighting alone. When we crossed into Iraq, we were only one of thousands of vehicles. The chaplain's Humvee was surrounded by M-1 Abrams tanks, Bradley Fighting Vehicles, artillery and air power as we set out to liberate Baghdad. In fact, a Bradley crew saved our lives in early April of 2003. We were part of a convoy on our way into downtown Baghdad when our soft-skinned Humvee came under attack from a carload of enemy combatants who fired at us as they approached. Before they could do any damage, a Bradley turned around and came back to our rescue and quickly destroyed the vehicle. At that moment, I was glad that I was a part of a combat team. I found the same to be true every day of my subsequent two years in Iraq and my nine months in Afghanistan. I never played the "Lone Ranger" as we never ever left our FOB by ourselves. I was always accompanied by my Soldiers and fire power at hand which was always greater than what the enemy could throw against me. To go it alone or to try to fight alone would just be stupid, foolish and deadly. Combat is no place to be alone.

The Army of God is also a "Combat Team..." Satan and his demonic terrorist forces are bigger and more powerful than we are whenever we try fight on our own, but when we band together in Christ, we are always assured of total victory. God's Combat Team has a better-known name: the Church. The church is not a building or a denomination. The Church is the people of God who, together, serve Christ as our true Commander-in-Chief. As Christian soldiers, we need each other for encouragement, accountability, fellowship, and sometimes even for spiritual protection.

Being a part of the Church is far more than just going to a church service in a building or believing in God. As a member of His church, we are a part of God's Army and His Family. We belong to Christ and we are all Christian Soldiers. God created His Church so we could grow in our faith through worship and hearing the Word of God but also so we could fight against the Devil as an effective spiritual combat team.

Satan knows that if he can keep us or convince us to go it alone that eventually we will become spiritually weak and vulnerable to his attacks. His goal is to make us will become a spiritual casualties so we are put out of action. Just as a lion stalks the weak and the stray, Satan also stalks the Christian who is not a committed member of a Spiritual Combat Team... So don't try to fight alone and end up wounded and a spiritual casualty. Join with the most powerful "combat team" in the universe by training/growing in faith, worshipping and fellowshipping with other believers.

BATTLE DRILLS:

Matthew 16:18-19: And I tell you that you are Peter, and on this rock I will build my church, and the gates of Hell will not overcome it. I will give you the keys of the kingdom of heaven; whatever you bind on earth will be bound in heaven, and whatever you loose on earth will be loosed in heaven.

1 Corinthians 12:27: Now you are the body of Christ, and each one of you is a part of it.

2 Corinthians 10:3-5: For though we live in the world, we do not wage war as the world does. The weapons we fight with are not the weapons of the world. On the contrary, they have divine power to demolish strongholds. We demolish arguments and every pretension that sets itself up against the knowledge of God, and we take captive every thought to make it obedient to Christ.

Ephesians 4:11-16: It was he who gave some to be apostles, some to be prophets, some to be evangelists, and some to be pastors and teachers, to prepare God's people for works of service, so that the body of Christ may be built up until we all reach unity in the faith and in the knowledge of the Son of God and become mature, attaining to the whole measure of the fullness of Christ. Then we will no longer be infants, tossed back and forth by the waves, and blown here and there by every wind of teaching and by the cunning and craftiness of men in their deceitful scheming. Instead, speaking the truth in love, we will in all things grow up into him who is the Head, that is, Christ. From him the whole body, joined and held together by every supporting ligament, grows and builds itself up in love, as each part does its work.

Colossians 1:18: And he is the head of the body, the church; he is the beginning and the firstborn from among the dead, so that in everything he might have the supremacy.

Colossians 3:15: Let the peace of Christ rule in your hearts, since as members of one body you were called to peace. And be thankful.

Hebrews 10:24-25: And let us consider how we may spur one another on toward love and good deeds. Let us not give up meeting together, as some are in the habit of doing, but let us encourage one another--and all the more as you see the Day approaching.

1. **What is the Church?**

2. **Describe the relationship between Christ and the Church.**

3. **What are some benefits of being a part of the Church?**

COMMO CHECK:

Talk to God and ask Him to help you find the chapel/church where He wants you to go and grow.

MRE: "Want To?"

I heard a story about two friends who decided to help each other lose weight. Their discussion went something like this: One lady called upon her weight loss partner and said, "Okay, this is what we will do. We will walk three miles every morning, count our calories, weigh ourselves once a week, and go to the gym three times a week. And if I call you because I get an urge to go out and get a hamburger, what are you going to do?" Her dieting partner responded, "I'll go with you!" I really doubt if this friend is going to help this lady lose much weight. Why? Not just because she lacks a plan, but because she lacks the desire and thus the discipline.

Many times we fail to achieve our goals or keep our commitments in life because we are not truly committed and lack the "want to." In those times when we struggle and fail, the best thing we can do is not give up, but to go to God for His help. The Apostle Paul tells us that the real motivation and might for change or growth is not found in our own willpower but in Christ and in His power. As a Christian, we really can live in freedom, make positive changes, keep our commitments, and we can grow spiritually. So, the next time you get tempted or get the urge to break a commitment, don't give in or give up, go to your Lord for His help!

"For it is God who works in you to will and to act according to His good purpose" (Philippians 2:13).

Medic!

(E-Encouraging Others)

In combat, one of the many often unsung Heroes are the Combat Medics also affectionately known as "Doc." Combat Medics are most often the first to render medical assistance to wounded or dying soldiers until the MedEvac arrives to fly or drive the wounded and dying out. I know of many soldiers whose lives were saved by Combat Medics, often under fire. Chaplains also spend much time with their Combat Medics. I rode with our Battalion Combat Medics all the way to Baghdad in 2003, after my own vehicle was destroyed. I ministered and served alongside our Medics, Nurses and Docs for 3 years as the Hospital Chaplain at Ft. Campbell, KY from 2004 to 2007. Finally, I responded along with our Combat Medics to our Forward Surgical Team (FST) as several hundred casualties received medical treatment and as 19 Heroes received honors in Hero Ceremonies. Combat Medics were and still are some of my best friends.

In the spiritual war on terror, every Christian Soldier is to be a Combat Medic. Life is not about me. The Christian life is about living for Christ and serving others. The more we do for God and for others, the more God blesses us and fills us with His joy. Every day we come into contact with people who are hurting and who are emotionally and spiritually wounded. We all constantly need help and encouragement. Many are bound by sin and stinging from the pain of failure. There are others whose lives and families have been devastated and whose dreams have been shattered.

You can be a spiritual Combat Medic. You can bring encouragement to the discouraged, and introduce them to Jesus who is the Great Physician. He can forgive their failures, heal their wounds, set them free, and put back together the broken pieces of their lives, marriages, and families which have been torn apart by Satan. To be a spiritual Combat Medic you must train (Bible study, worship, attend church/chapel, pray, be alert to the needs of others, and be willing to allow Christ to use you to reach out to others). One of the greatest feelings in the world is to know that God used you to help someone in need and to possibly help make an eternal difference in someone's life.

Every soldier must be trained, ready and willing to help a fallen comrade. No soldier should ever leave a wounded buddy behind and must do everything possible to save him or her. The same is just as true spiritually. Jesus left heaven, came to earth and laid down His life for us. Shouldn't we be willing to reach out to others? We must never leave a "wounded" Christian buddy behind but help treat their wounds and bring them back to the safety and healing of God's love.

BATTLE DRILLS:

John 13:34-35: "A new command I give you: Love one another. As I have loved you, so you must love one another. By this all men will know that you are my disciples, if you love one another."

Romans 12:10: Be devoted to one another in brotherly love. Honor one another above yourselves

Romans 15:7: Accept one another, then, just as Christ accepted you, in order to bring praise to God.

Galatians 5:13: You, my brothers, were called to be free. But do not use your freedom to indulge the sinful nature; rather, serve one another in love.

Galatians 6:1: Brothers, if someone is caught in a sin, you who are spiritual should restore him gently. But watch yourself, or you also may be tempted

Ephesians 4:32: Be kind and compassionate to one another, forgiving each other, just as in Christ God forgave you.

Ephesians 5:21: Submit to one another out of reverence for Christ.

Colossians 3:13, 16: Bear with each other and forgive whatever grievances you may have against one another. Forgive as the Lord forgave you...Let the word of Christ dwell in you richly as you teach and admonish one another with all wisdom, and as you sing psalms, hymns and spiritual songs with gratitude in your hearts to God.

1 Thessalonians 5:11: Therefore encourage one another and build each other up, just as in fact you are doing.

Hebrews 3:13: But encourage one another daily, as long as it is called Today, so that none of you may be hardened by sin's deceitfulness

Luke 10:29-37: But he wanted to justify himself, so he asked Jesus, "And who is my neighbor?" In reply Jesus said: "A man was going down from Jerusalem to Jericho, when he fell into the hands of robbers. They stripped him of his clothes, beat him and went away, leaving him half dead. A priest happened to be going down the same road, and when he saw the man, he passed by on the other side. So too, a Levite, when he came to the place and saw him, passed by on the other side. But a Samaritan, as he traveled, came where the man was; and when he saw him, he took pity on him. He went to him and bandaged his wounds, pouring on oil and wine. Then he put the man on his own donkey, took him to an inn and took care of him. The next day he took out two silver coins and gave them to the innkeeper. 'Look after him,' he said, 'and when I return, I will reimburse you for any extra expense you may have.' "Which of these three do you think was a neighbor to the man who fell into the hands of robbers?" The expert in the law replied, "The one who had mercy on him." Jesus told him, "Go and do likewise."

List the numerous responsibilities we have to one another as a Spiritual Combat Medic:

COMMO CHECK:

Talk to God and ask Him to give you opportunities to serve and help others today. Ask to be a blessing.

MRE: "To Protect and to Save"

I noticed something while on a run that helped me feel a little better. At about the 1 ½ mile point I passed a police station with seven patrol cars. On top of that blessing, about ¼ mile later I passed a fire station. Seeing the police station was a blessing because I knew if someone jumped me in the dark in order to steal my really cool New Balance running shoes, police protection wouldn't be far away. The fire station was a blessing just in case this old chaplain started having chest pains or fell and got hurt, medical assistance was also near. With this fresh assurance I was able to survive and finish a long and difficult run without incident or fear.

While the assurance of nearby police protection and medical assistance is helpful, having the assurance of God's presence, protection and care is far better. God is always with us, always watching over us and always right there with us. We don't even have to dial "911" and wait for God to show up! God never sleeps, has all the angels of heaven standing by to come to our aid, has all the resources of the universe at His disposal, and can move all of heaven and earth to come to the aid of one of His children in their time of trouble. So today, if you are hurting or feeling afraid, be sure to call on your Heavenly Father who loves you and is with you. He is ready to protect and to save. God always takes care of His children and He WILL take care of you!

"Praise be to the God and Father of our Lord Jesus Christ, the Father of compassion and the God of all comfort, who comforts us in all our troubles, so that we can comfort those in any trouble with the comfort we ourselves have received from God" (2 Corinthians 1:3-4).

Keep Up the Fight

(E-Encouraging Others)

The War on Terror is far different from any other war America has ever fought. Our enemy has little national loyalty and wears no uniform. The war has no frontlines and our enemy can strike at anyone, anywhere, and at any time. There can be no negotiations with terrorists because their goal is to kill us and/or kill themselves trying. Terrorists hope to totally destroy us and there can be no surrender. Our present War on Terror has no end in sight.

For soldiers, the War on Terror may mean long deployments, separation from family, many sacrifices, and months at a time in harm's way. As soldiers, we cannot quit in the middle of a fight, nor can we run in the face of fear or danger. We must fight on, we must endure, and we must remain faithful no matter the cost and no matter how long this war may rage on. Soldiers fight not only for themselves, but also for their buddies, for their families, for their nation and for millions of others who can't fight for themselves. Soldiers must keep up the fight.

The spiritual war on terror is also a different fight. Satan has only one goal in mind, to kill and to destroy. He can attack at any moment and usually does it when we are most vulnerable. We cannot negotiate, compromise or surrender. To do so only invites disaster. This spiritual war will continue to rage on as long as we live. As Christ's soldiers, we fight not only for ourselves; we fight for our God, our families and many others whose lives we may touch in one way or another. Christ's soldiers must fight on.

What is it that keeps us going when Satan attacks and the spiritual battle rages? What is it that helps us to get back up no matter how many times we may fail, fall or get hit? The answer is found in the abundant grace of God which we can receive new every day through faith. Faith in Christ is the essential weapon in winning the spiritual war on terror. Knowing that we are loved and forgiven no matter how many battles we may lose and knowing that God will never leave us or forsake us, especially in the middle of the battle, will sustain us until the end.

103

In our spiritual war on satanic terror, you don't have a choice. To quit or surrender will ultimately only bring misery, bondage and death. As you keep fighting, always remember, Christ has already won the war. You just have to keep on fighting until the end. A thousand past failures doesn't mean today can't be different. Every day is a new opportunity for spiritual renewal. Every day is a new beginning and a new opportunity to start over. His mercies are new every morning. His grace and love are always far greater than your sin. Today is the day to keep on fighting, keep on trusting and to enjoy the freedom you have already been given in Christ.

BATTLE DRILLS:

Matthew 10:22: All men will hate you because of me, but he who stands firm to the end will be saved.

1 Corinthians 15:58: Therefore, my dear brothers, stand firm. Let nothing move you. Always give yourselves fully to the work of the Lord, because you know that your labor in the Lord is not in vain

Galatians 5:1: It is for freedom that Christ has set us free. Stand firm, then, and do not let yourselves be burdened again by a yoke of slavery.

Galatians 6:9: Let us not become weary in doing good, for at the proper time we will reap a harvest if we do not give up.

1 Timothy 6:12: Fight the good fight of the faith. Take hold of the eternal life to which you were called when you made your good confession in the presence of many witnesses.

Hebrews 12:1-3: Therefore, since we are surrounded by such a great cloud of witnesses, let us throw off everything that hinders and the sin that so easily entangles, and let us run with perseverance the race marked out for us. Let us fix our eyes on Jesus, the author and perfecter of our faith, who for the joy set before him endured the cross, scorning its shame, and sat down at the right hand of the throne of God. Consider him who endured such opposition from sinful men, so that you will not grow weary and lose heart.

James 1:12: Blessed is the man who perseveres under trial, because when he has stood the test, he will receive the crown of life that God has promised to those who love him.

James 5:11: As you know, we consider blessed those who have persevered. You have heard of Job's perseverance and have seen what the Lord finally brought about. The Lord is full of compassion and mercy.

Revelation 3:12: Him who overcomes I will make a pillar in the temple of my God. Never again will he leave it. I will write on him the name of my God and the name of the city of my God, the new Jerusalem, which is coming down out of heaven from my God; and I will also write on him my new name.

1.   **According to these Scriptures, what are the benefits of staying in the fight?**

2.   **According to these Scriptures, what can help us to keep on fighting?**

COMMO CHECK:

Talk to God and ask Him to give the desire and the strength to keep on fighting no matter how many times you may fail. Thank Him for His grace.

MRE: "Grace"

Grace! Amazing grace! Wonderful grace! Abundant grace! God's grace! Not grace plus works, just grace. Grace and nothing else, just grace. How are we saved? Grace! How can we be forgiven? Grace! How can a God love us? Grace! How can we live as we should? Grace! How can we survive difficult times? Grace! How can we endure painful circumstances? Grace! How can we enjoy life? Grace! God's grace!

The sooner we realize that life is not about us and the sooner we realize that we all need God's grace, the better off we will be. The sooner we realize that we are totally helpless to save ourselves, to earn God's forgiveness, or to make it through life on our own, the sooner we can enjoy God's grace. How can we enjoy God's grace? All we have to do is ask. God will always respond with His matchless, abundant gift of grace to meet our every need. No situation is too difficult, no life too dirty, no problem too big, no hurt too much, or we can't fall too far that God's grace can't help, cleanse, solve, soothe, or reach. You will always find the greater your need, the greater and more amazing God's grace.

Remember the words of John Newton who was once a vile, slave ship captain:

"Amazing grace how sweet the sound that saved a wretch like me! I once was lost but now I'm found, was blind but now I see! Through many dangers, toils and snares I have already come. 'Tis grace hath brought me safe thus far, and grace will lead me home!"

If God's grace would send His Son to the cross for you, God's grace will always be there to help you!!

Homecoming

(E-Encouraging Others)

By far, the best part of any deployment is the homecoming. I have discovered that no matter how long I have been in the Army and no matter how many deployments I have faced, being away from my family never gets any easier. Almost every soldier has experienced the pain of saying "goodbye," boarding a plane and leaving their loved ones thousands of miles behind. I thank God for pictures, e-mails, phone calls and care packages, but most of all, I always look forward to going back home. There have been many times in my career that the hope and anticipation of going home was what kept me going in the darkest of nights and when physically, emotionally, and even spiritually I seemed to be running on empty. The joy of seeing the "Welcome Home" banners, hearing the band play and seeing the smiling faces of my family are experiences I will never forget.

One day, in our spiritual war on terror, we will finally be able to "pack up our gear" and go home to heaven. As much as we may enjoy our times down here, nothing will be able to compare to the celebration we will enjoy, the beauty and the fun of heaven. When we get to heaven, we will be welcomed by our "Commander-in-Chief" Himself, our Lord and Savior Jesus Christ. We won't be greeted by the music of an Army band, but the music of the band of angels and a heavenly choir. In heaven, we will finally be able to enjoy our families and true freedom forever and forever. We will never again have to endure the sting and pain of "goodbye," failure, sin, sickness or death, and our "reunion" will last forever. In heaven there is no more death, suffering, sin, pain, sorrow, or devil to attack us or our loved ones. In heaven, life (and us) will be perfect. In heaven, we will be rewarded, not with a Bronze Star, but with an eternal crown of glory. So, whenever you get tired of the fight, which seems to be going on forever, and life leaves you hurting, don't give up, don't get discouraged, just look forward to the joy of your homecoming and your reunion with Jesus Christ Himself!!

BATTLE DRILLS:

2 Timothy 4:5: 5: But you, keep your head in all situations, endure hardship, do the work of an evangelist, discharge all the duties of your ministry. 6 For I am already being poured out like a drink offering, and the time has come for my departure. 7 I have fought the good fight, I have finished the race, I have kept the faith. 8 Now there is in store for me the crown of righteousness, which the Lord, the righteous Judge, will award to me on that day--and not only to me, but also to all who have longed for his appearing.

Revelation 21:1-7: Then I saw a new heaven and a new earth, for the first heaven and the first earth had passed away, and there was no longer any sea. I saw the Holy City, the New Jerusalem, coming down out of heaven from God, prepared as a bride beautifully dressed for her husband. And I heard a loud voice from the throne saying, "Now the dwelling of God is with men, and he will live with them. They will be his people, and God himself will be with them and be their God. He will wipe every tear from their eyes. There will be no more death or mourning or crying or pain, for the old order of things has passed away." He who was seated on the throne said, "I am making everything new!" Then he said, "Write this down, for these words are trustworthy and true." He said to me: "It is done. I am the Alpha and the Omega, the Beginning and the End. To him who is thirsty I will give to drink without cost from the spring of the water of life. He who overcomes will inherit all this, and I will be his God and he will be my son.

What are the rewards we can look forward to when we have our homecoming in heaven?

COMMO CHECK:

Talk to God and thank Him for eternal life and for all the blessings of Heaven and eternal riches you have received through Christ. Thank Him for giving you such a bright future.

MRE: "Faithful to the End" (My Funeral Message for My Dad November 2008)

There have been many times, because I wear this uniform, that people have called me a "hero." While I appreciate their kind words; I always feel a little uneasy because in my mind, I am no hero. This morning, we are saying "goodbye" to a real hero, my hero, my dad. While my dad wasn't perfect and couldn't "leap tall buildings in a single bound," he was a hero in the eyes of his family and in the eyes of God because he was a true hero of faith. Because I was deployed to Iraq, I wasn't able to be there when my dad died, but far more importantly, I was there when he lived. In the Gospel of Matthew we find these words: "His Lord said unto him, "Well done, good and faithful servant; thou hast been faithful over a few things, I will make thee ruler over many things; enter thou into the joy of thy Lord" (Matthew 25:23).

My memories of my dad don't begin with my childhood, but six years before my birth. It was in February of 1955, when a drunk, who was "so low that even the dogs wouldn't even bark at him," walked down the aisle of a little Free Will Baptist Church in the mountains of West Virginia and was "born again." Just as the Apostle Paul shared his testimony of his conversion with everyone he met, including the guards who were "held captive" by his chains, we heard our dad tell his testimony of how he met Jesus, how Jesus saved his soul, his marriage and how Jesus called him to preach the Gospel. It may seem like a little thing that happened in February of 1955, but on that Sunday night, in that little church, Donald Trogdon, a 24 year old coal miner met Jesus and his life, our lives and the world would never be the same. A hero was born.

For the next fifty-three years, my dad faithfully served the Lord. He led my mom to Christ and eventually all three of us children became Christians. While Dad wasn't able to attend Bible College, may not have been a nationally recognized pastor or well-known evangelist, and never wrote a book on church growth, Dad faithfully pastored several small churches in West Virginia and Indiana. As I watched my dad work full-time, pastor full-time and serve God full-time, in both the good times and in the hard times, he taught me far more about ministry and the Christian life than I ever learned in a Bible College or a Seminary classroom. Dad taught me the "little things" by his life and his example. The most important of these "little things" was how to love unconditionally.

Dad was an example of unconditional love for his family, especially for my mom who he affectionately called, "LuLu" which was short for Loretta. Those who know my mom, know that at times, like all of us, she could be hard to love, but that never stopped my dad. He loved his Lulu. One of the many difficulties of watching both of your parents losing their battles with Alzheimer's, is seeing them wake up one day and realize that they don't know who you are, or they are or even worse, when they don't know each other. For the last year or so, Dad and Mom lived as strangers. That was until in September when I came home on R&R from Iraq. Dad had stopped eating, had lost over 45 pounds and was extremely weak. Even though he could barely stand up, he said something that surprised me and scared me a little when he asked, "Where is Lulu?" I walked him to the other side of the nursing home and watched him give his beloved Lulu a goodbye kiss. As I wheeled him back to his room in a wheelchair, I knew what I had just witnessed was a gift from God. Dad loved Lulu and Dad loved us. It may seem like a "little thing" but my dad is a hero because he loved his family and was faithful till the end.

Dad also loved the ministry. He worked in a factory and sold insurance just so the little churches he started and served could also have a pastor. He sacrificed so much, including time with his family, because he loved being a pastor to God's people. I watched Dad love God's people, at times whom, like us, who were hard to love. I watched him love people who hated him and love people who used him, but I also saw him love people because He knew that Jesus first loved him. We won't know how many souls were won to Christ by those who Dad led to Christ until we get to heaven. I do know for sure of his wife, his three children, his granddaughter, my children, my 2-year old grandson "Big Nate," who grandpa never seemed to forget and who is already practicing his preaching skills. I also know that every person God allows me to reach for Christ can all be traced back to the best and most loving pastor I have ever known in my dad.

My dad loved the ministry so much that he never really retired from being a pastor. The only way we were able to get him to walk into the assisted living facility, when him and mom couldn't live by themselves anymore, was to tell him that God had provided him with a "church" that needed a pastor. The salary wasn't much but did include room and board and came with a little "parsonage" room for him and mom. Dad was overjoyed and immediately started his new ministry. He walked the hallways, encouraged and prayed with his new "church members." He told me about how he led one elderly man to the Lord and I was amazed as I watched him take over a worship service from a local church and lead in singing and testimony time. Dad never stopped being a pastor and never stopped being used by God to be a blessing and to touch the lives of others. This was very evident when the facility later caught fire and the residents, including Dad and Mom, had to be evacuated to an empty church across the road. Guess what Dad did. He led all the other residents in a prayer and praise service! It may seem like a "little thing" but Dad was a hero because he loved the ministry and he was faithful to the end.

More than anything else, Dad was a hero because of his love for the Lord. Dad's love for Jesus motivated him in everything he did, his preaching, his singing and in his living. Dad's love for Jesus made sure that we had a Christian home. In our home, there were no cards, no cussing, no drinking, but there was Sunday School, Sunday morning worship, Sunday evening service, Wednesday night Bible Study, and mandatory church attendance any time the church doors were open. No excuse was good enough to keep us out of God's House. Today I am so thankful that I had a Dad who loved Jesus, not only on Sunday morning in church but every day of the week in our home.

Dad loved Jesus and never stopped loving Jesus. A couple of years ago, God gave me a precious gift. I sat in a doctor's office at the VA medical center I watched as Dad was given a memory test by a psychologist. Dad failed every part of the test. He didn't know the year, the month, his social security number, who was President of the United States or even where he was at. It was sad to see him so confused and struggle so. That was until the doctor gave him one last test. He said, "Mr. Trogdon, I want you to write down a sentence on this piece of paper. Write anything you want to write." I felt sorry for my dad and wondered what he would do until I, in amazement, watched him write, "I love Jesus with all my heart." The doctor was speechless and I was so blessed as I realized what a gift God had just given me. My dad had gotten the most important question of life right and had never forgotten it. It may seem like a little thing, but my dad is my hero because he loved Jesus with all his heart and was faithful to love Jesus till the end.

The best thing about being a hero of faith is not the promotions or medals we receive in this life, but in the eternal rewards we receive in heaven. Today our hearts are not broken because my Dad is dead because he isn't. We know that Donald Trogdon is not here in this casket, but he is in heaven with Jesus, with Jeanell and with all the other heroes of faith who have gone on before. Knowing that Dad is with Jesus and knowing that now

I have another reason to look forward to going to heaven myself, is what makes this a celebration of eternal life and not a funeral for the dead. A few nights ago, when Dad closed his eyes in death, he opened his eyes in heaven and saw Jesus face to face. Our hearts are broken this morning, not because my dad is dead but because we miss our hero, a true hero who was faithful in a few little things, but who is also being rewarded right now in heaven with the greatest things. Listen to the words of the Apostle Paul:

"For I am now ready to be offered, and the time of my departure is at hand. I have fought a good fight, I have finished my course, I have kept the faith: Henceforth there is laid up for me a crown of righteousness, which the Lord, the righteous Judge, shall give me at that day: and not to me only but unto all them also that love His appearing" (II Timothy 4:6-8).

I can just imagine grandpa right now up in heaven, asking God to watch out over Lulu and all of his family, singing and sharing his testimony and telling everybody he meets in heaven, including all the angels, that he loves Jesus with all his heart. Hopefully every one of us will, like Dad, be faithful in a few "little things" and hear, like Dad just so recently heard, the words of Jesus when He says to us, "Well done, good and faithful servant; thou hast been faithful over a few things, I will make thee ruler over many things; enter thou into the joy of thy Lord" (Matthew 25:23). Well done, Dad! We miss you and look forward to one day soon seeing our hero in heaven. You are and always will be our hero!

R&R

Rewind and Review

Review Questions:

1. List reasons why Believers need to read, study and know God's Word as a basic and daily discipline of the Christian life:

2. Why is it important for Christian Soldiers to be "Battle Buddies" to other believers?

3. What can a Christian Soldier look forward to at his or her "home-going" in 2 Timothy 4:6-8?

MRE: "God's Help for Your Heart Drive"

Several years ago, to my shock and surprise, I turned on my laptop to my email and was rudely greeted by a dark screen with an error message message informed me that the file needed to start my Windows XP was missing or corrupted. I did everything I knew to do. I restarted my computer, p F2, F8, F12, called all my computer nerd friends, and even talked to that Geek guy. I was faced with a choice. I could try to fix it myself and end up paying a money and lose everything on my hard drive (including my dissertation and a pictures of my grandson Big Nate) or I could call the Dell Support Hotline. I the right move and called the support hotline. A few days later, I received a rec CD and, with the help of an expert, I am now back online, surfing the net and de all my junk emails! I am also only using my IPAD to work on this study.

There are times in life when everything seems to break down because part of our lives is either missing or maybe even corrupted. We can do every we know to fix it ourselves but to no avail. We can call all our friends, wh experts at fixing everybody else's problems, or talk to someone who we think the "God Squad," and still nothing seems to work. We are then faced with a cl We can keep trying to fix our lives on our own and end up paying a high cos maybe lose everything, or we can call on God Himself for His support and God's "help line" is open for business 24/7 and you will never be put on hol designed your life and He can repair any problem, meet any need and help yc back up no matter how far or how many times you've fallen. So today, if your " drive" is locked up, a key part of your life is missing or you have been corrupt a "sin virus," call on God and He will help get you back up online. Don't forge loves you and He is the only One who can truly help you in your time of need

MILITARY PHOTOS

NATIONS TOGETHER

THANKS FOR THE SERVICE IN ALL WARS

ALWAYS PREPARED

MOUNTIANS EVERYWHERE

CHAPLAIN TROGDON POSING WITH CHILDREN

David K Trogdon, Chaplain (LTC), USA, Ret.

Made in the USA
Lexington, KY
06 December 2019